Write Now!

---

featured essays from the
University Writing Seminars
at Brandeis

2013–2014

Change the course.

Write Now! is a publication of the University Writing Program at Brandeis University. Correspondence and requests for additional copies may be sent to *Write Now!*, University Writing Program, Brandeis University, P.O. Box 549110 / MS023, Waltham, MA 02454-9110.

ISBN 13: 978-1-58390-153-3

Design and layout by XanEdu Publishing, Inc.. Printed digitally by Courier.

Photograph credits:

Cover photo by Sarah Seldomridge.

pp. 1, 3, 7, 9, 15, 17, 20, 22, 25, 28, 33, 35, 38, 41, 43, 46, 49, 53, 97 by Sarah Seldomridge. For more information about Sarah's photography, art, and design work, visit sarahseldomridge.com.

Acknowledgments:

pp. 54–95: From *Writing Analytically with Readings* by David Rosenwasser and Jill Stephen. Copyright © 2008 by Heinle/Arts & Sciences, a part of Cengage Learning, Inc. Reproduced with permission. www.cengage.com/permissions

p. 61: Whistler, James Abbott McNeill (1834–1903). *Arrangement in Gray and Black No. 1*, or *The Artist's Mother*. 1871. Oil on canvas, 144.3 x 162.5 cm. RF699. Photo: Jean-Gilles Berizzi. Musee d'Orsay, Paris, France. Photo Credit: Réunion des Musées Nationaux/Art Resource, NY. Reprinted with permission.

Change the course.

530 Great Road
Acton, Massachusetts 01720
800-562-2147
Visit our website at www.xanedu.com.

Acknowledgments

The Brandeis University Writing Program thanks Laura John, Katherine Nadeau, and Joanna Fuchs for their time and attention in spending many hours in reviewing essay submissions as judges of the student writing competition. We thank Lisa Pannella and Rebecca Mahoney for their ready assistance and sound advice in many matters. We thank also Acting Director of University Writing John Burt and Assistant Director of University Writing Nick Van Kley for insightful feedback and support of both the material and moral variety. Special thanks go to Susan Myrick at XanEdu Publishing for her patience, guidance, and encouragement. As always, we reserve special thanks for the instructors whose dedication and hard work continues to ensure the success of the UWS program. We thank also those instructors whose assignments and reflections appear here for their unflagging willingness to consent to our repeated requests for time and materials. Finally, we thank the students who find their work printed here for their readiness in responding to difficult editorial demands and for their enthusiasm in continuing the revision process beyond the bounds of the UWS course and the academic semester. About these contributing students and instructors, we can only say that it has been an incredible and inspirational experience to find solicitations for revisions and interviews made to so many on their own time universally met with such eager generosity. A greater pleasure we could not imagine.

We are also grateful to Thomson Higher Learning for allowing us to republish excerpts from *Writing Analytically*.

Contents

Introduction

Welcome to the 2013-2014 edition of *Write Now!*. I am honored and deeply grateful for the opportunity to bring to you this ninth edition of the Brandeis University Writing Program's annual recognition of the strongest and best student writing produced across University Writing Seminars during the past academic year. Once again, we've been fortunate enough to include as supplements to this edition generous selections from David Rosenwasser and Jill Stephens' *Writing Analytically*, an invaluable guide to drafting and revision. We are also extremely pleased to offer reflections from our featured authors on their own work during drafting and revision, along with comments from their instructors. Considered alongside the essays they describe, these reflections testify to their authors' investment in the revision process and their hard work in strengthening, expanding, and clarifying their arguments. First and foremost, *Write Now!* exists to recognize and celebrate this hard work, honoring what these students found themselves able to accomplish practicing the skills and methods of the UWS during a single semester. These essays and their authors will also be celebrated at the Brandeis University Writing Program's annual Celebration of Student Writing, and all will be entered into the next University Writing Program Prize competition, wherein the top three will receive special honors and win a cash prize. I heartily encourage everyone now holding this volume in his or her hands to join with me in recognizing these authors for their effort and accomplishment.

Our six featured essays replicate in miniature the cumulative experience of working through a University Writing Seminar, consistently employing the skills and methods that all good writing within the university requires while also confronting a variety of distinct essay types. Each of these types shares a need for analytic precision driven by a precise thesis, and in their variation we see the many tasks such work might serve. The volume begins with close readings from Sydney Miller and Jamie Wong, Sydney addressing a musical number from *West Side Story* while Jamie focuses her attention on one significant relationship within Peter Goldworthy's novella *Maestro*. Each close reading generates a specific, thoughtful thesis through extended attention to the finer details of its respective object of analysis, pointing out something significant about that object we'd miss without the benefit of that reading. Two lens analyses follow: one from Marc Fishbien using Kathryn Derounian-Stodola and James Levernier's account of Indian captivity narratives to read the film *Cowboys and Aliens*, and another from Hanchen Zhao that makes sense of the graphic novel *Watchmen* with Theodor Adorno's critical theory. Each lens analysis requires the same deliberate, extended analysis characteristic of the close reading, but here applied in a more particular way that demonstrates the utility of a particular lens or theory to make sense of a specific text. Finally, we present original research from Benyamin Mechede-Krasa and Daniel Leon. Research pairs the particularity of close reading with the need to establish an original historical or theoretical framework through which to understand a text, essentially a lens analysis the student constructs for him- or herself. In this case, Benyamin constructs an original entry into the existing body of scholarship on Philip Roth, one that follows from his reading of *American Pastoral*. Daniel's research in contrast develops an argument about the assumptions and beliefs built into the 2007 film *No Country for Old Men*, contextualizing it historically to produce a reading of its treatment of race and identity. In all cases, these essays stake out a specific realm for academic writing, that whatever the specific purpose it will remain particular, thoughtful, rigorous, and strongly motivated.

In each case, these essays demonstrate the best practices of the university and the habits that sound thinking has in common across the disciplines. Although their subjects differ significantly, each essay demonstrates the value gained from careful attention and thoughtful analysis. These essays, drawn from seminars in very different fields of study, demonstrate those qualities that good academic writing shares wherever it might appear. So too do these essays represent productive habits of mind in their engagement with drafting and revision. These final drafts represent what is possible within the context of a single course. Their authors worked to draft and refine these essays during a normal university semester, dividing their time and attention among all of the demands and responsibilities that crop up as the academic year rolls on. These authors gave only the time and attention that was available to them to spend, yet they produced superlative work as a result. The essays may not be perfect—and there is doubtless room for further revision with each of them, just as there is for all writing. Yet we can find models to follow and encouragement for future work in what appears here as a consequence of ready application of the methods of UWS. We take comfort in the knowledge that these authors drafted such productive and engaging arguments within the very real confines of life as students of the university. For this as much as anything, we are grateful to have these essays and to make them available.

Curious readers of all stripes should find much here to consider and much of value to take away. Preparing this volume for publication has been a great pleasure and an opportunity for which I am deeply grateful. I and everyone else at *Write Now!* hope that you find the experience of reading it a worthwhile one. We bid you all a hearty welcome.

Steven Plunkett
Editor, *Write Now!*

Write Now!

The Writer's Process—Sydney Miller

Sydney Miller approaches close reading as an opportunity to revise misunderstanding. The insights that follow from careful delineation of the fine nuances of and tensions within a text (be it an art object like "America" or an historical or sociological artifact like a ship's manifest or municipal building) sometimes find their most pointed use in correcting an overly simplistic assumption or a too-elementary reading. Writers often talk of this act of correction as establishing a motive, and it can come in more abstract or concrete terms. Writers sometimes approach the question of how to frame their reading in terms of the hypothetical—What might a reasonable person not realize at first glance? What did I miss two drafts ago?—or in more practical terms. Sydney approaches the argument through direct engagement with musicologist John Shepherd's claim that all music communicates through sound alone. Yet a too-narrow focus on rebutting or challenging some other argument often prematurely limits a close reading. Sydney remembers facing the question of how to balance close attention to the details of a text against the demand to frame a specific, motivated argument

> Initially, I found it difficult to develop an argument that entered into conversation with Shepherd's quote. Without even watching West Side Story, I became stuck on the idea that the only legitimate counter to this argument is that lyrics and sound make an equal impact when analyzing music, an argument that was not as original and complex as I would have liked. However, after watching the performance of the song "America" closely, I realized that instead of focusing on Shepherd's quote so intently I should simply concentrate on the musical to see what ideas come to me. It was after this that I realized how intentional every aspect of the performance was when relaying a message to the audience. I noticed how the choreography, costume, context, and lyrics work together with the music itself to give meaning to each of the songs.

This reciprocal relationship between the demands of a specific prompt and the rich detail of the text ended up allowing Sydney to answer Shepherd in a very full and nuanced way, returning to his narrow reading with a more detailed one partially by leaving his concerns behind and then using them to make sense of what she saw within the text. Throughout the drafting process, Sydney kept this notion in mind to sharpen her particular analytic claim

> In the conference, Professor Schwindt gave me tips on how to develop my argument to create a better flow to my essay. His most helpful tip was when he told me to restructure the paper so my argument remained in the foreground. Initially, my first body paragraph solely discussed how the sound of the song "America" sends a particular message to the reader. The following paragraphs then each examined the lyrics, context, choreography, and costume to show how they send a different message. Professor Schwindt pointed out to me that this structure actually weakens my claims by placing Shepherd's ideas in the foreground. He explained how my essay would be more effective if each paragraph contrasted a sound element with a non-sound element to demonstrate that the non-sound elements are crucial in relaying a message to the audience.

Joel remembers Sydney's approach as a productive one that engages the necessary elements of analysis within the university context, pointing out how Sydney meets the particular demands of close reading

> Right away, I was very impressed with her ability to seize on an interesting thetic [thesis-based] approach, as well as her ability to utilize her analysis to support her idea. In the conference, she asked insightful and important questions about my comments, but also had questions of her own. Her contributions in class were always strong, including what may have been the most challenging unit, namely how to use technical musical terminology to express your analysis in relation to sociological analysis.
>
> The foundation of all academic writing is finding a new idea to contribute. Not just analysis, not just observation, but a new way of looking at a subject. For this reason, the ability to not conceive and articulate a thesis was the most

important issue. Naturally, we focused on analysis, as well as the effective presentation of your idea through clear structural design (e.g., paragraph construction, topic sentences, examples, summary statements, etc.); however, without a strong idea to lead all of these elements, academic writing becomes either a simple "book report," or worse, a rambling series of observations

We are excited to share with you Sydney's close engagement with all of the relevant aspects of "America" as it appears within *West Side Story*.

Immigration, Assimilation, and Integration: Musical Analysis in *West Side Story*

Sydney Miller

When speaking of sociological issues in popular music, the scholar and sociologist John Shepherd asserts that, "any analysis of popular music as a cultural form must acknowledge that popular music makes its impact overwhelmingly as sound."[1] Although his claim addresses a critical aspect of analyzing popular music, he fails to account for other potential means by which popular music might communicate meaning. For example, *West Side Story*, an American musical set in the 1950s, explores timeless themes through its depiction of life in the West Side of New York City through the presentation of pop-musical songs presented within the larger context of a performed narrative. The musical examines the rivalry between two teenage street gangs, the Jets and the Sharks, each from very different ethnic backgrounds, addressing critical issues such as violence, love, immigration, and racism primarily through its incredible use of music. *West Side Story*'s form as an American musical means that each of its songs appears within the context of a larger narrative, each performed by characters with unique identities and specific stories, each of whom dress, move, and interact in particular ways that inform the music—all elements that escape Shepherd's characterization of popular music. The contextual background, choreography, and costume that make up much of theatrical music, particularly when representing sociological issues become of central importance when making sense of *West Side Story*. Through my analysis of *West Side Story*, I will examine non-sound factors, such as lyrics, context, choreography, and costumes in comparison to sound in the song "America" to demonstrate how the non-sound aspects of the song deliver a political argument specific to the time and place in which West Side Story is set, one that advocates assimilation. Through recognition of these aspects of the song, one will be able to gain a deeper understanding of Puerto Rican identity and other minority groups' perspectives in America, as well as an understanding of the significance of theatrical elements for the analysis of popular music within the form of the American musical.

While the rhythm in the song "America"—what Shepherd means when he describes "sound elements"—merely highlights the presence of racism in the character's lives, the lyrics assist in conveying a message to the audience, demonstrating that the primary focus of the piece is its patriotism. The sound simply exemplifies the tension between differing cultures in the musical. For example, "America" consists of mixed meter, having both duple and triple beats. This mixture of opposing beats emphasizes the combination of both positive and negative aspects of living in the United States. On one hand, America seems to offer countless opportunities for its citizens; on the other, various prejudices ultimately limit immigrants' abilities to enjoy them. This places emphasis on the discrimination that Latinos face in America. However, the combination of lyrics and sound discloses the possibilities that the United States has to offer. For instance, Anita first sings, "Puerto Rico, my heart's devotion," only to follow this line with "Let it sink back in the ocean."[2] Through the first two lines of the song, Anita

---

[1] John Shepherd "A theoretical model for the for the sociomusicological analysis of popular musics," in *Popular Music* 19, no. 2 (1982): 146.

immediately informs the audience that she despises her home country. She then portrays Puerto Rico as an underdeveloped country with multiple serious factors that impact quality of life: "Always the hurricanes blowing/always the population growing/and the money owing."[3] The fact that the song opens with the hardships that one faces in Puerto Rico suggests that the audience should focus on the positive aspects of America. Without the lyrics in the song "America," nobody would hear this message at all, his or her attention directed instead toward the tension expressed in the music's rhythm.

Not only do non-sound elements within the songs themselves communicate meaning, but the context in which the song appears--Anita's dialogue with Bernardo—also informs our understanding of it. Many readers of *West Side Story* consider "America" one of is most exciting and energetic pieces. Its upbeat rhythm and fast paced tempo make for a fun, lighthearted feel, which, ironically, contrasts with the serious and devastating message that it delivers. The juxtaposition heard through the music satirizes the patriotic comments made by Anita, diminishing the credibility of her praises for life in America. This places emphasis on the men's argument disparaging life in United States. However, similar to the lyrics, Anita's conversation with Bernardo reveals that the song seems to advocate for assimilation. When fighting for her friend, Maria, to love whomever she desires, Anita argues, "Girls here are free to have fun. She is in America now."[4] Anita is optimistic that America is a place of freedom for all. Soon after this comment, she mocks Bernardo's criticism of America, exclaiming, "Here comes the whole commercial. Your mother's a Pole, your father's a Swede. But you were born here, that's all that you need. You are an American. But us? Foreigners!"[5] In this comment, Anita shows her hope for Puerto Rican immigrants to truly be considered Americans. Just before the music begins, Bernardo calls Anita by her full name, Anita Josefina, but she quickly responds, "No, it's just Anita now."[6] Although her homeland is Puerto Rico, again she expresses her underlying desire to integrate as an American. This context within the larger performance has a significant influence on the representation of Puerto Rican immigrants' identity in America.

Choreography during "America" also informs an understanding of Anita's dominance of the scene and thus the larger debate about America. "America" switches from solos to ensembles throughout the piece. This inconsistency further highlights the incongruities between living in America as an immigrant and as a white man. However, this does not sufficiently account for what happens during the number. When one studies the choreography, however, he is able to see that Anita's arguments become the primary focus. For instance, while Bernardo lists criticisms of America during the number, emphasizing the economic inequality that the immigrants face, Anita walks away yawning, discrediting his claims. This sends a message to the audience that the men's arguments should not be taken seriously; rather, they should be brushed aside. In addition, during the instrumental, Anita kicks her feet in the direction of the men and aggressively shakes her dress toward them, once again demonstrating her opposition to criticisms of America. Here, Anita asserts her dominance through her body language, invisible to one only listening to the sound and lyrics of the song. Clearly, full sociological representation depends upon the choreography that accompanies the music.

---

[2] "America," from *West Side Story*

[3] "America," from *West Side Story*

[4] *West Side Story*

[5] *West Side Story*

[6] *West Side Story*

Another significant element of theatrical music, the costumes worn by the characters, illustrates Anita's desire to become homogeneous with Americans despite the message against immigration that the sound of the song seems to portray. While the conflicting harmonies in "America" parallel the conflicts that Puerto Ricans face, the clothing of the characters highlight Anita's desire to assimilate despite those prejudices. For example, Anita's dress resembles Latin American attire; however it appears to be Americanized. Puerto Rican dresses typically have elaborate ruffles, with the bottom half of the gown dramatically flowing outwards. While Anita's dress has ruffles, they are hidden under the top layer, only appearing when she dances or lifts up the edges. This symbolizes her desire to participate in American culture and to revise her identity in a more typically American way. The other women's dresses are also unruffled, portraying movement toward assimilation. Similar to the lyrics, context, and choreography in this scene, the visuals provide the reader with the central message that the song advocates for integration into American society.

As demonstrated, the electrifying music, brilliant lyrics, dialogue, choreography, and costumes used in the musical *West Side Story*, and specifically, the song "America" have added a new layer of meaning to the song's presentation of assimilation. When focusing simply on the sound of the music, the primary theme seems to be the discrimination inflicted on Puerto Rican immigrants in New York City. However, attention to other elements in the musical reveals another, contrary perspective. The female immigrants react to racism quite differently than the men, and express the desire to become Americans. By noticing all elements of the musical not communicated by music alone, the audience sees additional valences of an already intense story about belonging and discrimination. These findings do not only relate to *West Side Story*, but also allow one to gain insight into ethnic identity and the representation of sociological issues in popular music.

Works Cited

Shepherd, John. "A Theoretical Model for the Sociological Analysis of Popular Musics." *Popular Music* 2, "Theory and Method" (1982): 145–177.

West Side Story. Directed by Robert Wise and Jerome Robbins. United Artists, 1961.

Original Assignment—Close-Reading Essay

Course: Political Advocacy in the Broadway Musical: West Side Story
Instructor: Joel Schwindt

In our introductory discussions, we will be studying the use of musical dramaturgy to express, address, and represent sociological issues, in respect to John Shepherd's thesis (full article available on LATTE):

"Any analysis of popular music as a cultural form must acknowledge that popular music makes its impact overwhelmingly as sound."

In 5–7 pages, you will enter into a "scholarly conversation" with the Shepherd quote, based on your close reading of a single song or scene from *West Side Story*.

Please note: the prompt for this essay is brief and open-ended to allow you to be creative, a skill which is essential for academic writing. In other words, don't begin by asking, "what am I supposed to do?" Instead, study the musical closely and find a subject that speaks to you, in keeping with the guideline(s) offered in the prompt. The pre-draft assignments, which are based in non-thetic analysis, are designed to help you to home in on a topic choice for the essay.

The Writer's Process—Jamie Wong

Sometimes, effective close reading requires judicious selection of relevant evidence pulled from a much longer text with much more going on than a single essay can describe. Jamie Wong faced such an issue with her close reading of Peter Goldsworthy's 172-page novella *Maestro*. Although not particularly long in an absolute sense, the text still offered Jamie far more potential passages, characters, events, and themes to consider than she could hope to analyze in six pages. "It was hard for me," she recalls, "because in the beginning I didn't know what to focus on." Fortunately, Jamie made use of instructor Georgia Luikens's assignment sequence to set for herself some specific questions to consider and patterns to follow, which Jamie describes below

> The course is divided into units, and the units helped me along. Georgia told us that she wasn't going to just give us the prompt and expect an essay from us, so the steps she set up helped us along. I wasn't sure where to start because I had read through the book, and even though the close reading what a type of essay I had done before, there's a different level Georgia was expecting here and I wasn't sure how to meet it. But I figured out through the unit process what to do. We were first asked to take selections from the text, and then to analyze those on our own. It became a sort of process we could use to figure out our ideas. And for me, the way that I usually figure out how to find a topic for an essay or for an assignment is to find a parallel or a theme that I like. Doing the minor assignments helped me to focus on one. And the passage that I chose for one of the short assignments ended up being the one that I chose for the essay. Having those shorter assignments really helped.

Jamie's attention to the advantages offered by out-of-class analysis and pre-draft assignments gave her the advantage of posing specific questions of the text as she prepared for class, setting her up to approach the assignment with a sense of what threads she wanted to follow in crafting her close reading, and especially of what evidence she wanted to use in the development of her thesis. Georgia agrees that close-reading a longer text requires this specific sort of effort

> Often you'll have students starting a close reading assignment by saying, "this is such a short text. I can't possibly write six pages about it." With the novella, we ran into the opposite problem. This is such a long text: how can I possibly fit everything into five or six pages?" The students who were successful had to throw out the desire for a holistic understanding of the entire novella and everything in it: they had to focus on what they saw as being the most important aspect and how it fit into the larger picture. It can be overwhelming when the students see it and think that there's too much to handle, that there's just too much material. How can you choose what is the most important?

Jamie's particular work at that step resulted in particular consideration of the relationship between the novella's protagonist and another major character, following the significance of one particular interaction—both how it follows from what happens before and how it informs what happens afterward. Jamie explains her approach

> My essay focuses on Paul and Keller's potential relationship. In the drafting process, I had to explain to Georgia what I meant by that—but as I read I noticed the two of them coming together, and to me it was a point in the plot of the book where those characters were close and then they start to drift apart afterwards. So then I wanted to explore how it was a lead-up to a point where after that the plot heads somewhere else. Afterward, Paul leaves and it takes a very different direction. I wanted to focus on that one point and I wanted to bring identity into it, which was the purpose of the assignment in the first place.

Georgia describes her experience of working with Jamie and her ideas, what it was like to encounter the efforts Jamie mentions above, and what advantages of those efforts became evident in her rough draft as a result

I think that because she had such an in-depth knowledge of the text, she could really narrow her attention to what she wanted to focus on. The degree of thoroughness and depth of engagement with the characters and situations really stood out to me. She brought in the idea of values, which was very interesting. She tried to integrate different ideas of identity in the first draft. It was still a very good draft, and you got the sense that it was really draft number three. And so the rejiggering that took place was fairly minor for the final draft. The reasoning behind the thesis became stronger. Having a thorough knowledge of the novel and really being interested in bringing something of her own to her reading of the text made a real difference.

We hope that you find Jamie's close reading as engaging and clear as we did, and that you can see the marks of careful consideration and early analysis on the draft Jamie shares with us here.

Adelaide: The Pinnacle of
Paul and Keller's Potential Relationship

Jamie Wong

"What is the difference between great and good pianists?" (31). Keller's question, introduced in the beginning of the novella *Maestro* by Peter Goldsworthy, initially frustrates Paul due to his perceived inability to bridge the gap between "great" and "good." *Maestro* covers themes of music and life through the growth of Paul Crabbe from adolescent to adult. The novella focuses on the relationship between Paul and his piano teacher Eduard Keller, a famous musician and Holocaust survivor. Paul and Keller start as strangers with conflicting musical values, such as what makes a great musician, but their relationship progresses into a stronger bond beginning in the Intermezzo and ending in Keller's eventual death. However, the only point within the novella where Paul and Keller's agendas and mentalities meet is when they unite to practice for Paul's piano competition in Adelaide. In this period of time, Paul and Keller's musical values finally intersect because in their efforts to reach a common goal (Paul's success) they both make adjustments. Once united, their relationship strengthens to the point where Keller even offers to teach Paul for many years and turn him into a "great," rather than a "good." musician; Keller's offer, the culmination of their work together and Paul's performance in Adelaide, is the pinnacle of their potential relationship. In order for Paul and Keller to reach that level of unity, they first must reconcile some of the differences in their approaches to music.

Paul begins his lessons with Keller as a young, arrogant, and emotional student who refuses to understand Keller's cryptic words or his critical attitude. One of their early conflicts is when Keller insists Paul practice and relearn *The Children's Bach* rather than begin with advanced pieces. Paul claims that "it's easy" (27) while Keller claims the exact opposite, "Bach is never easy" (27), which is a clear example of one of the fundamental differences between their approaches to music. Alongside Paul's arrogance is his pursuit of fame and attention, which is shallow and fueled by his desire of instant gratification. The pursuit in question would be satisfied by Paul's success in the other musical competition in his life, the Battle of the Sounds. In addition, Paul's intensifying relationship with Rosie becomes more important than focusing on his studies. Based upon what was known of Paul before practice begins, his arrogant demeanor, shallow pursuit of fame, and budding love for Rosie, one would think that Paul would prioritize the easy success in the Battle of the Sounds and Rosie over practicing for a piano competition with Keller. However, Paul's values change and intersect with Keller's once they begin to practice for Paul's piano competition.

During his first period of intensive practice with Keller Paul, similar to Keller, begins to value music above all else. "I also was hungry—I had not eaten—but there was no informing Keller of such trifles" (99). This line sounds like a statement that Keller would support rather than Paul, but in actuality it was stated by Paul. For Paul, hunger becomes an insignificant trifle brushed aside for a productive session. Paul's adjusted values change his previous arrogant and self-centered behavior. Even more telling is when Paul asks himself,

> How could I tell him that I planned a different sort of practice ,that I needed to write out new chord changes and bass riffs for Reelin' and Rockin'? I could not even have told him that I needed to study for

school exams: Differential Calculus and *Great Expectations* and Garibaldi's First Landing on Mainland Italy. All of this was, suddenly, nothing. (99)

All of Paul's priorities, clearly listed so it is apparent that they are important enough to be remembered, become insignificant when juxtaposed against the prospect of practicing with Keller in order to reach their common goal. Rather than compromise or pretend Paul discards them as nothing. Paul realizes that it would be ridiculous to tell Keller of these insignificant stressors and his own reaction matches how he thinks Keller would react. Paul dismisses his own hunger and other influences in his life to focus on practicing and as a result he better understands Keller.

Paul's increased understanding of Keller strengthens their bond. If Paul did not place the same amount of focus and importance on their practice as Keller does, he would not have discovered new information about Keller. In Paul's quest to learn more about Keller and his past, he collects any clues relevant to what Keller's feelings may be. After their first practice, Paul notes that it was "a clue that his contempt for teaching music to me was just another charade. Clearly he didn't have to teach. His contempt was fuelled by feelings far more complicated and contradictory than I had thought" (100). This is the point in the novella where Paul begins to understand that there are other, more personal, reasons for Keller's overcritical behavior. At first glance the revelation may not seem significant but it is one piece of many that push forward *Maestro* in terms of plot progression and character development—or, since the novella is written in Paul's perspective, the discovery rather than the development of Keller's character. Like Paul, Keller also adjusts his values, thus strengthening their bond by allowing the practice for Paul's piano competition to occur.

Keller is expected to hold disdain for musical competitions. Before Keller decides to help Paul practice for the competition in Adelaide, he visits Paul's household and disapproves of Paul's playing of Beethoven which he claims is "Technically perfect [. . .] And yet something was missing. Not much—but *something*" (46). According to Keller's judgment of how Paul played, Paul is only a 'good' pianist rather than a 'great' one because of the small difference that Paul fails to recognize. Keller marks Paul as only technically perfect, a description that would hold no sense of disapproval if it wasn't for Keller's continued criticism. It can be assumed that Keller at that point did not believe that Paul had the potential to become a 'great' musician. However when the topic of the piano competition in Adelaide comes up, he agrees to help Paul practice. Assisting Paul goes against all that is known of Keller so far; not only does Keller disapprove of how Paul plays he also disapproves of the basis on which competitions and their judges function. Keller states that "They seek athletes, not musicians. They judge a scherzo with a stopwatch" (97). Here, Keller introduces the dichotomy of the athlete versus the musician; he is a firm believer in the musician who has the small difference that turns a 'good' musician 'great' and rejects the athlete who seeks technical perfection in quantifiable standards. According to Keller's critical attitude towards Paul's playing up until that point, Paul would fit the description of the athlete rather than the musician.

Yet, Keller decides to practice with Paul for the competition in Adelaide as musicians. "'We will go one better,' he smiled grimly. 'For them we pretend to be athletes. For ourselves, we play music—at the same time! We win the race, and we also keep our self-respect'" (97). One of the most important aspects about Keller's statement is his use of "we" because it shows how he treats himself and Paul as a unified group of likeminded individuals rather than the two separated men they once were. Keller rationalizes their participation in the competition by differentiating them from the rest of their competitors; they, not us, are the athletes that the judges look for and Paul and Keller will win by disguising themselves among the lesser musicians. By creating reasons for Paul to enter the competition and for he himself to commit to practicing with Paul, Keller shifts his own values in order to share a common goal with him. It can also be seen that winning the race and keeping his self-respect is held on the same level for Keller, while Paul is still more concerned with success rather than the respect that Keller treasures.

However, their goal is still the same and the elements of the athlete—Paul—and the musician—Keller—meld together in their practice session. The Scherzo is split into parts: "This part is not for the stopwatch. More a... slow bike race. [. . .] You must keep the hands still, the bicycle balancing with nothing but nerve" (98). The scherzo is divided into stopwatch parts and non-stopwatch parts, the stopwatch being the pure technicality that Paul once focused on. Keller's description of how to play the part of the musician, incorporating that element that separates the 'good' from the 'great', uses language that strays into figurative territory rather than technical terms that would dictate an academic lesson at the Conservatorium. In addition, the comparison of playing the notes to riding a bicycle is one that is seemingly personal to Keller because of how he asks "Do you [Paul] have them [bicycles] in this country?" (98). So, Keller is asking Paul to draw upon his own memories while revealing another bit of information about himself and his own past. These snippets of information strengthen the bond between Paul and Keller and mark the beginning of the new, improved, stage of Keller and Paul's relationship.

In *Maestro* the competition in Adelaide is not the beginning or the end of Paul and Keller's relationship. The beginning is the Intermezzo when Paul receives Keller's gift and the end is when Keller passes away. However, the competition in Adelaide is significant in how it was the pinnacle of their potential relationship. Paul and Keller's potential relationship refers to what connection Paul and Keller could have had if the events in the book transpired differently. In this context, it refers to the launch off point where their relationship could have developed further if Paul decided to take the chance to continue to study under Keller as his pupil rather than enrolling in Adelaide. Paul gains the opportunity during his dinner with his parents and also discovers that Keller believes Paul was the best pianist there (113). While Paul did not achieve material success by winning the competition, their relationship developed and he convinced Keller that he may have the potential to close the gap between good and great. For both Paul and Keller, their matching musical values enabled them to finally understand each other and reach the point in which they could have forged the strongest bond possible.

"'What is the difference between a great and a good pianist?' I asked him, repeating one of his favourite questions. 'Not much,' he admitted. 'Little bits'" (113). The exchange between Keller and Paul on the night Keller offered to turn Paul into a great musician highlights the stark difference between then and now. Then, when Paul did not understand the "little bits" Keller spoke of. And now, when Paul repeats his question in agreement and wishes to learn the "little bits" from Keller rather than create conflict on what the little bits are or on what Keller's intentions were. Despite how Paul does not take Keller's offer and join him against the wishes of his parents, the piano competition in Adelaide marks the culmination of all the practice and progress made between them. Through the lens of Paul and Keller's potential relationship, Adelaide is the only point in which they could have created the strongest bond between pupil and Maestro.

Works Cited

Goldsworthy, Peter. *Maestro*. North Ryde: Angus & Robertson, 1989. Print.

Original Assignment—Close-Reading Essay

Course: Stories from the Piano Bench: Fictional Narratives of Musical Life
Instructor: Georgia Luikens

Through the close reading essay you will learn how to analyze a text to find deeper meaning. In this and all other essays you must construct a thesis and present a strong argument in defense of your thesis. This assignment requires an in depth analysis of an extract from Peter Goldsworthy's novella *Maestro*. The extract you select will obviously need to support your reading of the issues in response to the essay prompt. A principal goal (and perhaps challenge!) of this essay is to combine an analysis of these elements and reflect on them analytically, without simply summarizing the action taking place and/or scholarly materials that have been published on the work in question. Once you are clear of your interpretation, you must then provide supporting evidence.

In this assignment sequence, you will learn how to close read a written text. When you close read, you focus on noticing facts and details of the whole text, or a specific portion of the text, that leads you to draw conclusions about the whole. Close reading is a detailed observation of patterns in a text which, after analysis (i.e. the interpretation of your observations based on sound evidence), leads to intelligent and exciting conclusions.

Not surprisingly, close reading is a skill that is extremely important for writing academic essays across the disciplines.

NB – no outside sources should be used in this essay.

Essay Prompt

The novella Maestro reflects certain axioms of musical identity through the protagonists Paul Crabbe and Eduard Keller, including the parallel dichotomy of the "Genius Maestro/teacher figure with a secret" and "inspired yet misunderstanding (and perhaps misunderstood? pupil." The ways in which these two constructs create various tensions throughout the novella invite the astute reader to question the ways in which musicians are depicted in fictional works.

How are the musical identities of Paul Crabbe and Eduard Keller presented in Peter Goldsworthy's novella *Maestro*? How do their identities as musician interact with their emotional lives and their relationships with others (including each other)? How are these presentations used to drive both form and function of the broader elements (plot, characterization, tone/style, theme/s, setting) of the novella?

The Writer's Process—Marc Fishbein

Lens analysis often provides the opportunity of revealing more about a focus text than may be apparent, demonstrating the significance of textual details we likely wouldn't think twice about or even notice without the lens text's narrow and particular perspective. In Marc Fishbein's case, writing about the 2011 film *Cowboys and Aliens*, he noticed right away what his lens text might reveal. Derounian-Stodola and Levernier describe how American captivity narratives of the nineteenth century represent Native Americans. In this the lens text uncovers the assumptions and unselfconscious attitudes of the people writing these nineteenth-century narratives, but Marc saw immediately that it could do the same thing for the twenty-first-century *Cowboys and Aliens*, a text that according to his essay seems to self-consciously avoid the racist tropes of older western stories. "*Cowboys and Aliens* tries to avoid the innate racism of other stories, and in that it's a product of its time—trying to avoid obvious racism in that way," says Marc of the film. Yet his argument demonstrates very clearly that at the same time *Cowboys and Aliens* cannot escape the basic narrative of dangerous barbarians threatening civilization, one that Derounian-Stodola and Levernier describe. The great strength of Marc's argument comes from his demonstration that an attempt to eliminate harmful ideas case repeat it. "The lens [text] can account for all that," Marc says "even though their approach is entirely historical." For Marc, the lens text's utility comes in its ability to reveal ideas the film seems to ignore or criticize.

Marc describes the effort he expended in getting his argument to the point of revealing the film's inability to escape presenting a dangerous, alien "other" that opposes civilization, saying that he found it no easy task. "The initial draft wasn't very specific," says Marc, "and it was probably a few pages short of the minimum," addressing only how the aliens behave like the American Indians of the classic western narrative. Waiting for revision were his more spectacular claims that the aliens also embody cultural elements associated with white Americans—and that the film ends up excusing its white characters of their greed, lust, and violence by assigning those characteristics to the aliens. Speaking of his revision process, Marc describes how peer review with fellow seminar members and conferencing with his instructor, Nick Van Kley, each informed his approach to his argument

> Peer review was when I first started realizing how superficial the original argument was. It helped to highlight the problems with the original thesis, and the later conference helped me to identify ways to fix those problems. Nick's help was a big part of this. That's really where the argument expanded into what it is now. We went over the film to look for more specific examples beyond what was present in the draft. In the conference we expanded on the main idea and got to the thesis as it is now. We focused on making the thesis more complex, of hitting on the issue of how the aliens also do things that resemble what the white settlers do in Derounian-Stodola and Levernier's lens text. We found more ways to complicate that original thesis.

Nick likewise describes the work Marc set for himself in revision, framing larger questions and beginning to think them through during their conference together

> In our conference, we talked about developing ideas that would stitch Marc's local claims into a more unified, motivated argument. We were particularly interested in asking what it meant that the film resembled and departed from the radition of the Indian Captivity Narrative. We asked what the film was asking its viewers this feel about the history of white American expansion in the 9th century and how that feeling was related to 21st century racial politics.

Both Marc and Nick appreciate the need to engage the full possibility of what the lens offers the focus text. "It's easy to treat the dialogue between the case and the lens as an exercise," he says. "The best essays manage to make the connection between the case text and the lens text seem vital and organic without making it also seem predictable." Marc's own description of developing his claim as fully as it appears in his final draft stresses this element of his lens analysis, which itself follows from his work at revision. His final draft forcefully interrogates *Cowboys and Aliens* with a particular purpose in mind, something Nick calls possible because of Marc's engagement with motive

Marc's essay was exception precisely because he was able to generate a more powerful motive than many of his peers. The points of connection between the case text—a somewhat dry history of the "Indian Captivity Narrative" genre from the colonial period to the 19th century—and the film were easy to locate for many. But not many students were able to explain to readers why those points of connection produced a unique and important insight that extended beyond the walls of the classroom. In drawing a connection between the lingering features of the Indian Captivity Narrative in *Cowboys & Aliens*, attending the peculiarities of the film's adaptation of that tradition, and explaining what these aspects of the film suggest about contemporary American racial politics, Marc generated an exceptional motive. His essay stands out because of it.

We invite you to discover the full force of Marc's demonstration of *Cowboys and Aliens*'s participation in the *Indian Captivity Narrative.*

Celebrating the Ends to Justify the Means

Marc Fishbein

When one thinks of the old west in media images of sheriffs, outlaws, and Indians are all conjured. The film *Cowboys and Aliens* contains these yet also adds a modern twist of science fiction with the inclusion of alien invaders. Yet the themes, tropes, and motifs this movie draws upon are old, centuries old in fact, and Kathryn Derounian-Stodola and James Levernier's book *The Indian Captivity Narrative, 1550-1900* chronicles and scrutinizes many of the stories, historic and fictional, which gave rise to those themes, tropes, and motifs. *The Indian Captivity Narrative* argues that within American history the Indian captivity narrative served multiple goals of white society ranging from wartime propaganda to creating a sense of American national identity. The film *Cowboys and Aliens* retains the structure of an Indian captivity narrative as foundational to American national identity while unsuccessfully attempting to remove the elements of racism towards Native Americans pervasive in the Indian captivity narrative. Specifically, this film affirms the narrative of triumph over the wilderness through the characterization of the aliens as savages, substitutes Native Americans for aliens as the uncivilized other, yet also gives the aliens attributes of white society which serves to reverse to roles whites played in the history of westward expansion, which has some disturbing implications. As fictional creatures that threaten all of North America's historically real inhabitants, the aliens seem the perfect means to cast both American Indian and white American as equals united in defending the continent, yet collecting the worst traits of both peoples within one fictional culture both preserves the distorted notion of the barbaric, alien Other and absolves the historical Americans of the nineteenth century of their crimes against the Native Americans who shared their continent.

Indian Captivity Narratives documents how American media representation categorizes Native Americans into two groups—good Indians and bad Indians—and explains how this image serves the changing needs of white society. Derounian-Stodola and Levernier make the claim that "recent anthropological and historical studies have noted that two distinct images of Indians predominate in white American culture from colonial times through the present: one negative and one positive" (52). They go on to describe the two depictions. Bad Indians are "portrayed as culturally and often mentally deficient and incapable of what white society considered civilization and progress [. . .] simply put [. . .] barbarian" (52) while the good Indian "opposes what the 'bad' Indian represents" (52) and often sides "with the values of white society" (52). To summarize the two images, bad Indians are violent savages and what makes good Indians good is that they do what white culture tells them to do. Derounian-Stodola and Levernier examine the purposes such ideas serve for white society. The dual image of Native Americans portrayed in captivity narratives function as propaganda for the "essentially expansionistic, white, agrarian society that needed new territories as it grew in both size and military strength" (53) to justify their actions. Those actions entail the removal of "the 'bad' Indian, whose unwillingness to adapt to European cultural norms necessitated a policy of extermination" (53) and of the good Indians who "also became expendable" once they had "served their purpose" of "assisting in colonization" (53). *Indian Captivity Narratives* stresses that colonization is the goal of white society and anything that stood in that path must either assist it or be destroyed.

Cowboys and Aliens affirms the narrative of triumph over the wilderness through victory over a savage enemy, sending signals about white colonization very similar to the traditional captivity narrative. In this film the enemy are aliens; in captivity narratives the enemy are Indians. Derounian-Stodola and Levernier give examples of bad Indians as unreasonable savages, inferior to white society, something that must be conquered for civilization to expand. Science-fictional aliens usually appear civilized and physically frail, their technology looking clean and polished. In this film the alien invaders are nothing like that. Physically they appear somewhat like a cross between a lobster and a gorilla, and their technology and behavior seem reminiscent of animals as well. Their large spaceship looks like some kind of beehive and the smaller craft look like dragonflies. In combat the aliens fight primarily by running on all fours and then tackling people and biting them or slashing them with claws. Although the aliens all have guns strapped to their arms, they hardly ever make use of them in combat, preferring claws and teeth. The existence of futuristic weaponry the aliens have at their disposal combined with their apparent refusal to use it adds to the image of barbarity. The characterization as savage animals matches Derounian-Stodola and Levernier's image of bad Indians in captivity narratives that have no place in or desire for settled or sophisticated society.

If aliens are a force of chaos, what must be their fate? In *Cowboys and Aliens* the hostile aliens, like the image of bad Indians, cannot be reasoned with and must be destroyed. The aliens, as far as is shown in the film, cannot speak and even if they could would likely not negotiate. The survival of the aliens means the extinction of humanity and so they must be destroyed, just like the bad Indians. The Indians hinder white settlement and cannot become a part of it. The parallel become unmistakable. This shows how *Cowboys and Aliens* serves to enforce the narrative that the expansion of civilization requires the elimination of the barbarian outsiders and the results of that policy can be seen in the film. At the end of the movie the once terrorized town is happy and wealthy—the aliens defeated—their newfound wealth following from seizure of gold the aliens had earlier mined. One character mentions that the now-peaceful town will soon join a larger network of railroads uniting the west. The railroad is a sign of the more refined culture of the east and when it arrives it brings developed eastern civilization along with it. *Cowboys and Aliens* preserves this specific narrative, that the growth of civilized white culture requires the suppression of disruptive outside elements.

Although *Cowboys and Aliens* contains many of the elements and messages of the Indian captivity narrative it makes a conscious effort to avoid the racism present in historical Indian captivity narratives. Contemporary Americans have made this film, far removed from a time of direct conflict with Native Americans or wartime propaganda. Now political correctness is the norm and self-conscious audiences meet racism with vocal and widespread disapproval. The movie's implicit understanding of this appears in the first scene where Jake, the protagonist played by Daniel Craig, wakes up in the middle of a wasteland, confronted by bounty hunters. Jake soon kills these men and takes their belongings, but the audience knows to take Jake's side and feel no remorse for the bounty hunters: the film identifies them as villains through close-ups of the Indian scalps in their possession, which to a modern audience immediately identifies them as bad people deserving no sympathy in their racism and complicity in genocide. *Indian Captivity Narratives* describes this sort of changing attitude toward American Indians: "No longer a military threat, the Indian, together with the frontier, was perceived as a rapidly vanishing national heritage that needed immediate preservation" (168). Replacing Native Americans with aliens as the enemy of the expansion of civilization allows *Cowboys and Aliens* to tell an old story without offending a modern audience with racist caricatures of Native Americans.

Cowboys and Aliens shapes the Indian captivity narrative for a modern audience even further through piling onto the aliens not only the worst features of the caricature of the savage Indian, but also the worst excesses of the expansionistic Americans. Serving not only as stand-ins for violent Indians, the invading aliens also appear as militaristic and wealth obsessed as the nineteenth century's white settlers. The aliens, we learn, invade Earth in pursuit of gold, the same motive many of the movie's settlers have for expanding into new territory and exploiting new lands. The aliens perform medical experimentation on their prisoners though the application of sophisticated technology at odds with their otherwise animalistic behavior. This sort of violence comes from a technologically advanced society which Europeans are viewed as and Native Americans are not. The medical experiments the aliens perform on their captives look like modern western medical practices as they involve instruments, such as carefully laid out scalpels and bright lights, which would not look out of place in a modern hospital's operating rooms. This serves to further contrast the aliens against Native Americans as Native American medicine is usually portrayed very differently involving ritual and herbs. Equating the aliens with white settlers flies in the face of Indian captivity narratives which almost exclusively show a white perspective. In this film the aliens are the antagonists and so their actions are condemned and that condemnation carries over to what the aliens represent. By having the aliens represent the violent expansion of white society *Cowboys and Aliens* condemns it. This modern perspective adds to its narrative a condemnation of conquest and destructive westward expansion.

Yet just as the film attempts to give a more nuanced commentary on history through the role reversal of whites and Native Americans through the violence of the aliens it also fails to recall the historical reality that Native Americans are largely the victim of expansionist white society. By making the aliens the violent aggressors the film casts the white settlers, not the Native Americans, as victims. While the aliens attack both Indians and whites, the audience sees practically none of the alien's violence towards the Native Americans and the film focuses almost exclusively on the whites. This robs Native Americans of legitimate claims of victimization. *Cowboys and Aliens* tries to have its cake and eat

it too. It abandons many of the racist images of Native Americans but keeps the structure and message of the stories that use them; it characterizes the aliens as both uncivilized savages and as invading imperialists, and it casts white society as both victors and victims. Overall there is a massive cognitive dissonance present in the film as it both praises and condemns the American method of westward expansion. The question then arises of how the movie can have such a fundamental contradiction and still make sense.

Cowboys and Aliens answers that question through the character of Jake. Jake is the protagonist of the film and he has amnesia. Both Jake himself and the audience know nothing about his past and must discover it as the film progresses. Jake eventually learns that he is an outlaw who has killed and stolen in the pursuit of personal wealth, yet the film still sympathizes with him as he continues to engage in violent acts. Hiding Jake's past from the audience prevents them from immediately judging him as a bad person and not caring about what happens to him in the future. Also the film easily justifies all of the violence the audience sees him perform explicitly within the narrative. From the very beginning of the film where Jake kills some bounty hunters, he does so because they threaten him directly—these bounty hunters visually coded as evil and immoral, which justifies Jake's actions toward them. This theme of forgetting past evil deeds appears once more at the end of the film where the sheriff accepts Jake into the community because of his help in defeating the aliens, his past as an outlaw forgotten once again. At the end of the film the movie as a whole seems to have a similar amnesia. The film ends happily. The barbaric aliens defeated, the townspeople now enjoy their newfound golden wealth as civilization continues to expand westward. These people and perhaps the audience too easily forget that the aliens were just as gold-hungry and ruthless as the settlers are in their expansion. The violence of westward expansion drops away, all earlier crimes forgiven, while the film praises the results of that violence. In this final respect *Cowboys and Aliens* mirrors the Indian captivity narratives exactly.

Cowboys and Aliens ultimately retains the structure and message of an Indian captivity narrative even as it reflects modern sensibilities. *Cowboys and Aliens* celebrates the triumph of white society over the wilderness and its barbarous inhabitants by casting the invading aliens in the role traditionally played by Native Americans in Indian captivity narratives and defeating them yet does so without casting Native Americans as villains. It condemns the violence of westwards expansion by condemning the actions of the invading aliens and giving them attributes and motives common to white settles but by doing so overshadows the real historical suffering of Native Americans with this fictional victimization of white settlers. Overall *Cowboys and Aliens* praises the results of westward expansion while half-heartedly condemning its methods. The issue of Jake's amnesia when extended to the larger issue of historical perspective is particularly interesting. It is very easy so see the results of historical events from the present but it is just as easy to forget the suffering that led to them. Could this film have done more or is there something inherent to the western genre that leads to this issue?

Works Cited

Cowboys and Aliens. Dir. Jon Favreau. Perf. Daniel Craig, Harrison Ford, Olivia Wilde.   Universal Studios Entertainment, 2011. Film.

Derounian-Stodola, Kathryn Z., and James A. Levernier. *The Indian Captivity Narrative: 1550–1900.* New York: Twayne U.a., 1993. Print.

Original Assignment—Lens Analysis

Course: The New Old West
Instructor: Nick Van Kley

Develop a 7–9 page argument about the recent Hollywood film *Cowboys and Aliens* using one or more of the ideas you encountered in our readings from the Kathryn Derounian-Stodoloa and James Levernier's book *The Indian Captivity Narrative, 1550-1900*. Identify one or two aspects of the Indian captivity genre and use them to analyze, illuminate, or interrogate some aspect of the film.

In their study Derounian-Stodola and Levernier trace the role of the captivity narrative in the national history of the United States. The excerpts we are reading explore how these stories produced images of native people that served specific political purposes at different moments in American History. Readers were sometimes invited to revile the Indian captors as savage brutes in order to justify their extermination. At other times, readers were invited to sympathize with them as practitioners of a more "natural" culture in order to support nativist rhetoric. At still other times, readers were meant to mourn the supposedly inevitable loss of a noble native culture. As stories of intercultural encounter, captivity narratives functioned as tools for white Americans to understand and shape their relationship to native people and to the frontier.

Cowboys and Aliens (2011) mixes many common themes and storytelling techniques from both Westerns and Science Fiction. It is also a captivity narrative. Using the ideas about the depiction of Indians in captivity narratives that you gather from reading Derounian-Stodola and Levernier's book, make an argument about how Cowboys and Aliens adapts the captivity narrative tradition. A few questions you might ask:

What particular techniques seem borrowed from the captivity narrative tradition? What is the effect of creating a third identity category (in addition to "white settler" and "Indian")? Who occupy the positions of "natives" and "settlers" in this story? Why is it important that the captive in this story has amnesia? Who are we meant to sympathize with in the film and why?

There are obviously many differences between the film and the captivity narratives written over a century ago. You may choose, ultimately, to focus on any number of differences and similarities, provided that your thesis addresses the following questions in some way: What do the film's representational strategies invite us to think about the expansion of American Empire in the 19th century? How does the film seek to re-vise our understanding of "Manifest Destiny" and White-Native relations?

Writing Goals: As always, the essay should pursue a unified thesis, which will, of course, prevent you from addressing all of the questions above. The essay should also offer a compelling motive, use both paraphrase and quotation to relay the ideas in Derounian-Stodola and Levernier, offer sustained analysis of close textual detail from the film, and pursue a developmental structure. I will also look to see you experiment with your conclusion in a way that addresses our conversation about conclusions from this unit.

The Writer's Process—Hanchen Zhao

Sometimes, the power of a lens text comes not from the variety of arguments it suggests at first glance, but from the careful work of thinking carefully and seriously about how its vocabulary and perspective might inform a text that seems very distant from its concerns and questions. For Hanchen Zhao, making the Frankfurt School critical theorist Theodor Adorno speak productively about 1985's science-fiction graphic novel *Watchmen* seemed a difficult task. Adorno's text addresses the reception of art in Weimar-era Berlin, dividing art critics into separate categories on the basis of how they understand their own relationship to the music and paintings they evaluate for a popular audience. Hanchen worked to find ways of making this particular argument speak to *Watchmen*'s murder-mystery plot. "For the art part," says Hanchen, "it's really not that helpful for talking about *Watchmen*." But he noticed quickly a wider relevance for Adorno's specific argument

> Maybe there is some contemporary meaning that only works for that period [Adorno's own pre-war context]. There are still deeper ideas that can work in all times, then or now. That's the most important part of an article like Adorno's, that it can have constant value—it can have a lot of functions: different people can use it in different ways beyond the uses its original author had in mind.

Hanchen set about gaining hold of that more constant value by taking a careful look at Adorno and thinking about his premises, vocabulary, and assumptions. "Kurt asked us to talk about the general idea of each paragraph of the Adorno. Many of us had trouble doing that for some paragraphs, but for the paragraph I focused on I was able to come up with a good answer. I think Adorno's big ideas are not really that hard to get at, he just lays them out in a way where they're not always clear." Hanchen worked deliberately and methodically to seize upon Adorno's more valuable concepts, and found ready application for them once he had isolated them

> Once you understand the transcendental critic, and that such a person can only see the world in absolute good and absolute bad with no middle ground or third category, things stick out to you. Kurt asked us to come up with several words to describe each character in Watchmen. For Rorschach I came up with the most words by far. He's rigid, with a black-and-white worldview. He categorizes people into two absolute categories. He's almost too perfect of an example to describe the transcendental critic. At first, I came up only with the idea that Rorschach is the perfect transcendental critic. Later, I came up with the idea that the ending of Watchmen implies something very specific about the ultimate fate of the transcendental critic. At the end, he makes this really strong demand that somebody kill him—he says, "Kill me!" He cannot accept any defect and so he cannot live in a world more complicated than his way of seeing.

Thanks to this careful approach to Adorno, Hanchen saw real and meaningful avenues into *Watchmen*, Adorno's critical vocabulary opening up a fictional narrative once Hanchen went to work seeing who else aside from a German theatre critic might count as a transcendental one. Kurt Cavender, Hanchen's instructor, describes Hanchen's work from his point of view

> Hanchen was extremely diligent about taking advantage of office hours and the Writing Center on this assignment. He came to my office hours 5 or 6 times, first to make sure that he really understood the Adorno lens text, and then to discuss his ideas about its application to Watchmen. He really took the initial idea of the prompt and made it his own. It was Hanchen's own early idea to read Rorschach as a cultural critic, and to understand the contradictions of his position in terms of the contradictions Adorno outlines in the article. I was very impressed [. . .] I think the real hidden danger of the lens text the temptation to argue that the primary text does or does not agree with the lens. The difficult move is to push beyond this simple identification of agreement or discord, and ask why it this is significant or useful to note. What do we gain from thinking about the primary text in these terms? The temptation for Hanchen

would have been merely to point out that Rorschach disagreed with Adorno and was comfortable making transcendental claims; his success was in moving beyond that to show how the contradictions immanent to Rorschach's position (which Adorno helps us see) reflect back onto the text itself as well.

Hanchen also describes his work with consultants at the Writing Center to keep pushing his analysis forward, noting that the collaborative environment there can help with brainstorming and drafting and not only discussion of complete drafts

> I can't tell you how many times I went to the writing center. I went to see Matt [Writing Center Consultant Matthew Schratz] every week and talk about the progress of my essay. One of the most impressive comments Matt made was about Rorschach's gloves, that he says that his gloves are spotless even though they're very dirty. Matt and I talked about that and we realized that Rorschach speaks about contamination of his rigid ideas as dirt, and actual dirt doesn't matter to him. He helped me to realize my ultimate claim, that it's not real dirt Rorschach mentions.

We hope that you find the finished argument provocative and illuminating. Hanchen really demonstrates both the value of thinking carefully about how to use lens texts and the rewards that come with careful and deliberate revision and reflection. Certainly, in his case that rigor and care has produced a provocative, daring argument about the worldview of Watchmen and its characters.

Black and White: What It Means to Be a Transcendent Critic in *Watchmen*

Hanchen Zhao

A utopia is a community or society possessing highly desirable or perfect qualities. It is an ideal place in which evil does not exist and good fills the whole world. But is it possible for a utopia to become real? In "Cultural Criticism and Society," Theodore Adorno introduces the idea of transcendent criticism, a type of cultural criticism which idealizes the notion of utopia. People taking the transcendent approach attempt to criticize a culture from the outside and try to set up an objective view. In order to do this, they mechanically categorize their objects and divide the world into black and white, that is, good and bad or right and wrong. In *Watchmen*, a graphic novel written by Alan Moore and Dave Gibbons, Rorschach embodies this transcendent criticism, and thus functions to demonstrate its limitations. In the novel, he manages to find out after a long investigation that Ozymandias has killed fellow costumed adventurer the Comedian. However, the Comedian's death is the consequence of his own discovery of Ozymandias's plan to end the Cold War by faking an alien attack that destroys New York. In the end, Rorschach refuses to condone Ozymandias's plan, even though it might save the world, and asks Dr. Manhattan to kill him. Why is Rorschach unable to accept this plan? Why does he beg Dr. Manhattan to kill him? By depicting Rorschach's seemingly objective view towards people and his machine-like categorizing approach to ethical decisions, Moore makes Rorschach a perfect model of transcendent criticism, and demonstrates that although transcendent criticism might work as an appealing theory, one cannot translate it into a coherent practice.

According to Adorno, transcendent critics tend to criticize their objects mechanically and divide the world into two extremes. As he writes in "Cultural Criticism and Society," transcendent critics "forget the effort of conceptualization required and content [themselves] instead with the prescribed label" (Adorno 33). They criticize their objects based only on the common sense established in their society, and as a result never generate their own intellectual products. Instead of taking their prescriptions from the specific situation, they distribute their ready-made labels to the objects of their analysis. According to Adorno, these critics divide the world into "black and white [. . .] with the aid of mechanically functioning categories" (Adorno 33). They operate just like machines, sorting good and bad and transporting them to their right place. Transcendent critics label an object either as "white" or "black," and for them there is absolutely no ambiguity. This means, for Adorno, that transcendent critics "know the place of every phenomenon and the essence of none" (Adorno 33). They are aware of good and bad as they understand them. However, they have no idea why something is good or why something else is bad. The good, they simply celebrate; the bad, they simply denigrate.

Not only do transcendent critics categorize their objects like machines but they also do their job without considering the context of their objects. Instead, the critics unconsciously relate the objects to critic's own context. Adorno argues that transcendent critics "buy up culture en bloc from society, regardless of the use to which it is put" and "lack the experience of that with which they deal" (Adorno 31–2). In other words, they never care about the context of the objects that they criticize, instead offering a preprogrammed answer no matter what the object is, just like a judge makes his final decision on a criminal. They are only capable of surface level observation, and as a result apply criticism not to the actual object, but only to its most obvious effects. This means that these critics can never understand the object itself because they only evaluate it on their own, often inappropriate, terms. Adorno suggests that this produces a "paranoic system of delusions which is cut off from experience of the object" (Adorno 33). This means that as transcendent critics neglect experiences of their objects, they unconsciously substitute their own experiences instead. They often think of their frightening experiences, and the dark shadows in their hearts result in their delusions from time to time. As Adorno points out, no object is "safe from perversion into delusion once it has renounced a spontaneous relation to the object" (Adorno 33). These delusions have a great impact on their views towards their objects as well as their decisions to categorize their objects.

Rorschach from *Watchmen* is an ideal model of the transcendent critic. He sees the world in black and white and categorizes people like a machine; in doing so, he refuses to consider the context of his objects while unconsciously relating them to his own private experiences. Rorschach notes in his journal that "there is good and there is evil, and evil must be punished. Even in the face of Armageddon I will not compromise in this" (Moore 1.24). In his eyes, no qualified state exists between pure good and pure evil. People are all divided into these two groups, which seem like two extreme poles. Conceiving of himself only as a mechanism to punish evil, he maintains very rigid ideas and will never change them no matter what happens. No one can stop him because he has internalized the task and cannot separate himself from it. According to his algorithm, he can only repeat the same instructions, and punish evil whenever he sees it. Furthermore, once someone commits evil, Rorschach will always consider them evil. For example, even though the long-retired criminal Moloch wishes only to live a peaceful life alone, Rorschach still continuously hassles him. Moloch is so afraid when Rorschach visits him that he cannot stop sweating. However, Rorschach remarks only that his sweating "looks unpleasant" and pushes him into the refrigerator (Moore 5.5). Although sweating is a normal physiological response to stress, Rorschach, already seeing Moloch as evil, considers this an inevitable sign of guilt, and tortures him with threatening behaviors. Also, his rigid mind explains why he cannot accept Ozymandias's attempt to save the world by destroying half of New York City. After Rorschach learns everything related to Ozymandias's plot, he says "never compromise" and walks out without hesitation (Moore 12.20). Even though Ozymandias succeeds in ending the Cold War, Rorschach still regards him as evil and cannot stay silent because Ozymandias's solution automatically falls into his "black" category. Instead of considering both the good and bad sides of Ozymandias's solution or responding to it in pragmatic terms, he only sees the deaths caused. Like a robot, he always completes his task, without thinking about the implications.

In addition, Rorschach categorizes people only on specific actions, without consideration of the context behind them. As shown in *Watchmen*, although Moloch tells Rorschach that he "spent the seventies in jail" and is "not Moloch any more," Rorschach still categorizes him as "black" and treats him as a criminal (Moore 2.21). Moloch has served his prison sentence, and thus already "paid" for his crimes. However, Rorschach is not interested in that context at all, and believes that Moloch still needs to be punished because he did evil things before. In Rorschach's eyes, evil people can never fully pay for their mistakes and always deserve more punishment. Similarly, after Rorschach finds two dogs gnawing on a human bone, he kills the dogs with a meat cleaver. When the dogs first see him, they are represented as non-aggressive: they stick their tongues out and their ears cock up with a black background (Moore 6.21). This response reveals their innocence; they have no idea who they are eating at all and only know they have been fed meat. The black background implies that Rorschach has already put them into the "black" category. He never thinks about whether the two dogs are aware of who they are eating, or if they are ethically accountable. Instead, he regards them as "black" and kills them simply because they are gnawing on the human bone.

Interestingly, although Rorschach does not take his objects' context into account, his views towards them are affected by his own historical context. We see through flashback that Rorschach grew up in a single parent family and his mother was a prostitute. Since his mother saw her son as an encumbrance, she constantly showed "resentment and cruelty" to him (Moore 6.30). His childhood is full of sex and violence. Instead of being taken care of by parents, he lacks parents' love and his heart is full of dark shadows caused by his mother. He describes a nightmare he suffered when he was thirteen: he had "dirty feelings, thoughts and stuff" when he woke up and the dream "physically" upset him (Moore 6.32). He was only thirteen at that time, but he was already having sex dreams that aroused his dirty thoughts and made him feel sick. This reveals that his mother's prostitution has a great impact on him and stimulates his sensitivity to sex, while also driving him to feel shame about this sensitivity. These past experiences result in delusions from time to time. As Rorschach notes in his journal, after he sees Dreiberg and Juspeczyk leaving dinner together, he suspects Juspeczyk of having an affair and engineering Dr. Manhattan's exile to make room for Dreiberg (Moore 5.11). It is very common for opposite sex friends to have dinner together; however, Rorschach immediately thinks of an affair and suspects an outlandish conspiracy plot. He has no context to help him understand what he sees; all he knows is that Juspeczyk leaves dinner with Dreiberg. He unconsciously interprets this phenomenon according to his own context and concludes that he must investigate further. This faulty logic shows how his root of delusions affects his views towards even his friends.

As a transcendent critic, Rorschach always categorizes people in a detached way. As noted by Dr. Malcolm Long, when Rorschach learns of his mother's brutal murder, his only comment is "good" (Moore 6.8). When a normal person learns his mother is killed, he can expect to feel extreme sorrow or anger. However, Rorschach in contrast becomes surprisingly calm, even glad. Even his mother is not exempt from his objective categorizing rule. In his eyes, his mother is in the "black" category because she prostitutes herself and constantly treats her son with cruelty. As a result, he thinks his mother's murder is what she deserves. Interestingly, Rorschach describes his dirty gloves as "spotless" (Moore 5.18). His ironic description of the gloves implies that his idea of what it means to be dirty does not involve real dirt, but rather contamination through departure from his rigid ideal. It doesn't matter why people do what they do or what else they do, only that they deviate from his absolute standard. Remarkably, his black-and-white mask can change its pattern from time to time (Moore 1.12). Although the pattern varies all the time, the black-and-white color never changes. This implies that he always holds an objective view and sees the world in black and white no matter what happens.

In order to stay objective, Rorschach feels obliged to rid himself of emotions and separate himself from society. However, Adorno's claim that "the choice of a standpoint outside the sway of existing society is as fictitious as only the construction of abstract utopias can be" suggests it is impossible for people to get rid of the effect of society, because they are all products of society and can never live outside it (Adorno 31). As Rorschach tells Dr. Malcolm Long, after he killed the two dogs, "it was Kovacs who said 'mother' then, muffled under latex. It was Kovacs who closed his eyes. It was Rorschach who opened them again" (Moore 6.21). Calling "mother," crying, and closing his eyes reflect his fear and pity in front of the frightening dead dogs. However, he believes that Rorschach, as a true transcendent critic, should have no subjective emotions. Since that version of himself who closed his eyes was driven by emotions, he is not, according to Rorschach, truly Rorschach yet. Similarly, when he later returns to his apartment to get his things back, he meets his landlady and says: "told press I'd made sexual advances to you. Not true. Very bad" (Moore 10.6). No emotions can be seen from his short black-and-white comment. Instead of getting angry at the fact that the landlady spoke negatively about him, he puts her into the "black" category only because she lied. He does not care about her negative comments since he sees himself outside society and can never be affected. However, he does not realize that it is impossible to completely separate himself from society.

We see the limitations of this kind of transcendent criticism most clearly in the way the novel represents Rorschach's death. Before Rorschach leaves for Antarctica, he writes in his journal that "whatever precise nature of this conspiracy, Adrian Veidt [Ozymandias] [is] responsible" and drops his journal into the mail box (Moore 10.22). All of his observations and thoughts throughout his investigations, as well as his entire transcendent theory about the ethics of Veidt's plan, are included in his journal. In the final moments of the novel, we see that his journal is successfully delivered to a publication and is about to be revealed to the world (Moore 12.32). This creates a problem. Ozymandias has united the world by destroying half of New York to make people believe they were attacked by aliens. As long as people do not know the truth, they will only see the good result that the Cold War has ended. However, after reading Rorschach's journal, the public will discover the truth and know how "black" Ozymandias is. Instead of only seeing the result, people will also realize how bad the process is: half of New York was destroyed. The implied success of Rorschach's transcendent approach, then, is its ability to change the public's ethical understanding of the event. But the weakness also becomes clear: Rorschach is unable to change people's actual behavior. I have to think like him already in order to see Ozymandias as a villain.

Ultimately, even though people read Rorschach's journal and discover the truth, they can do nothing but to stay silent. In the end, Rorschach realizes this himself, and begs Dr. Manhattan to kill him (Moore 12.24). Ozymandias's destruction of half of New York automatically falls into Rorschach's "black" category. In his eyes, Ozymandias is definitely evil and must be punished. His transcendent approach obligates Rorschach to fight against him and to tell people the truth. However, if he manages to tell people the truth, then world peace will end and the nuclear war will start again. Since revealing the truth would cause numerous people to die, truth itself falls into the "black" category. As a result, neither of the choices available to him can work without violating his transcendent theory. Only death can allow him to remain a perfect model of transcendent criticism that, as he asserts, "never compromises" and always sticks to his transcendent theory (Moore 12.20). However, Rorschach's companions are not so rigid as him. They understand that if they do not stay silent, then world peace will end and humanity will suffer from the nuclear war again. The best choice for them is to stay silent, because half of New York has already been destroyed and they can do nothing to change this fact. Furthermore, they understand that the only solution to the dilemma faced by anyone who accepts Rorschach's theory is to die. People are not purely transcendent as Rorschach and tend not to value rigid theory more than their lives. Unlike him, the other humans who populate the novel are driven by more complex reasoning and emotions. Although their view towards the event may change, they will still find the ethical justification to stay silent by thinking about implications rather than stick to the rigid rule mechanically.

Adorno helps us to understand the characteristics of a transcendent critic, while Rorschach uses his life to illustrate what it means to be a true transcendent critic. As a transcendent critic, he sees the world in black and white and categorizes people as if he were merely a robot; as a transcendent critic, he disregards situational context and instead clings to an extremely objective view; as a transcendent critic, he tries to separate himself from society but in doing so ignores the fact that he is the product of society. His fate tells us that transcendent criticism might succeed in affecting how people think but necessarily fails in affecting how people act.

Works Cited

Adorno, Theodore. "Cultural Criticism and Society." *Prisms*. MIT Press: 1981. 19–34. Print.

Moore, Alan, and Gibbons, Dave. *Watchmen*. N.Y.: DC Comics, 1987. Print.

Original Assignment—Lens Analysis

Course: Living in the End Times
Instructor: Kurt Cavender

Theodor Adorno has suggested that art after the Holocaust is no longer capable of 'making sense' of the horrors of modern social reality. Alan Moore's graphic novel *Watchmen* presents a set of characters, each of whom represents a different ethical framework as they struggle to come to terms with first the threat and then the reality of an apocalyptic event. In this second assignment, you will use Adorno's essay "Cultural Criticism and Society" as a lens to analyze, in a 6–8 page paper, one of the ethical models offered in the text as it struggles to 'make sense' of the text's horrors. Your aim is to synthesize your understanding of Adorno's argument with your understanding of specific ethical systems represented in the text in order to create an argument you could not have made through close reading alone.

Goals of the Essay

Open with an engaging introduction that makes the motive of your essay clear. Recall Gordon Harvey's description of motive as "the intellectual context that you establish for your topic and thesis at the start of your essay, in order to suggest why someone besides your instructor might want to read an essay on this topic or need to hear your particular thesis argued—why your thesis isn't just obvious to all, why other people might hold other theses that you think are wrong." As of your thesis: "So what? Why would someone care? What's unexpected here? How is this interesting?" until you can respond with a satisfying answer. The answer will lead you to your motive. Underline your motive in all drafts and revisions of this paper so it can be quickly identified.

Create a dialogue between two texts. Don't settle for a baseline reading of the points of connection between *Watchmen* and Adorno's essay. Rather, devise a thesis that identifies how (and how well) Adorno's argument works as a lens to explain the form and function of ethical dilemmas in the text. You will also want to identify a "twist," a place where your case and lens don't match up perfectly. This is your opportunity to revise, refine, or even critique Adorno—you need not agree with him wholeheartedly, just remember to explain why you disagree and to logically examine merits and faults. Essentially you are being asked to both interpret the story and reflect on your lens. As always, close readings of specific passages are required to support and/or complicate your argument.

Grapple with Adorno's ideas, rather than taking isolated passages out of context to support your ideas. Whenever you are called on to bring a critical text into an assignment, your essay will not only be judged on the merit of your original ideas but also on how accurately you represent and make use of the critical text. Even when you disagree with the author, you must explain why you disagree, and that requires you to fully understand the author's position to begin with. When you refer to Adorno, make sure you engage his main ideas and not a side ideal.

The Writer's Process—Benyamin Meschede-Krasa

Research as framed within many disciplines requires on the one hand attention to the existing scholarly conversation, while on the other demanding a heavy emphasis on the skills of close reading to develop an original claim capable of entering the scholarly conversation. Benyamin Mechede-Krasa balanced these two imperatives by using his research as a means of shaping the questions he wanted to ask with his project, beginning with a broad topic that allowed him to shape his inquiry through what he discovered. Ben explains his process

> I had the hardest time picking a topic for that essay especially. I started off with a very broad conception, and that was how Ms. Minder [Ben's instructor, Orah Minder] introduced it. I pulled the theme of identity from a list of very broad topics to begin, and when I did my annotated bibliography I looked up a lot of articles about the novel that engaged that idea. I was able to draw specific ideas from articles that weren't exclusively about identity—the separate articles together look unrelated in some ways, but they could often inform my project because the topic of identity is so broad. It's easy to get caught up in focusing on a super-specific idea that's already been talked about. Not committing to a specific idea right away helped me to come up with a more useful, specific thesis.

Beginning from this perspective, Ben was able to link his interest in how the characters of American Pastoral think about identity and the formation of identity to some ideas already circulating in Roth scholarship. "The scholarly conversation already said something about food and the consumption of food," says Ben. "One was very general, all about Roth's treatment of food everywhere, in his fiction and his writing about his own life. Another was more specifically about American Pastoral." Drawing on this interest, not all of it having to do explicitly with identity, Ben gave focus to his own argument and applied his own close reading skills to develop a more specific argument. "I noticed I could tie that sort of thing into an argument about identity," he says.

Orah Minder, Ben's instructor, also notes the strength of Ben's analytic focus, and the way it follows from his engagement with the larger body of scholarship

> There's close reading all over this essay. In my experience, that's something students struggle with in research. I think there's close reading in every paragraph. This draft brings two characters together and really reflects the scholarly conversation. Ben makes a very clear case for how his own argument fits into the conversation. The essay shows a concerted effort to help the reader follow the argument. That's partially about topic sentences—at no point do I get confused about where the essay's going. He brings his reader with him as he goes. There's a paragraph where he's discussing Byland's discussion of Merry's consumption of food, where he frames that argument and then presents his own argument. I can hear his voice in that paragraph alongside what Byland says. In the first half of the Byland paragraph he says "here is how I'm using her ideas to develop my argument" and the second half says "and here is how I'm adding something to that argument." He wouldn't be able to make his argument if he weren't engaged so clearly in Byland and didn't have such a precise command of her argument.

Such a balanced application of close reading operating alongside a larger scholarly discussion follows from serious effort at revision, and both Ben and Orah put particular focus on revision as essential for research. "One great strength that Ben brought to the entire semester was a willingness to realize that drafts are a necessary step in the process of coming to a final draft," stresses Orah. "In his thesis, it's very clear to me that it reflects the entirety of that drafting process. That thesis is very complex and very innovative. It's very clear that he's using his skills from the other assignments as well." For his part, Ben describes the ways in which getting through that revision can frustrate, or generate uncertainty

> In general, especially with this essay and its drawn-out process, I had put in a lot of time and energy and still didn't necessarily have a great idea of where it was going. I had a lot of ideas and I just couldn't draw all the connections.

It was a little less organized than I was used to with other sorts of work or other essays. With my close reading, I was on top of it—I had a draft a week before it was due. I had a solid idea with the lens before it was due, but this time I had a much harder time with planning. I definitely drew on close reading—that's something I always did, that I had gained previously. The lens essay set me up well to engage the scholarly context. It was different because here there was a lot more of your own perspective against the lens.

Yet like many of our other featured authors, Ben found conferencing with Orah a helpful experience in developing his argument and putting all of his close reading to productive use

All of the conversations I had with Orah were very helpful. In the drafting process I am always very skeptical of my own ideas. I felt like I was all over the place and was very skeptical about what I had in some places. I always came out of those feelings a lot more relaxed and confident that it would all come together. Just bouncing ideas off of each other in conversation helps a lot—a lot of how I think it just out loud, bouncing ideas around.

Ben's process reflects the possibilities of engaging a larger conversation as a place to begin, both its considerable advantages and a potentially intimidating uncertainty that may arise. Yet Ben's story confirms that we can best understand this uncertainty as a single step in a larger process of analysis and revision, one that ultimately enables compelling and complete finished arguments.

Activity and Passivity in Relation to Environment

Benyamin Meschede-Krasa

Identity is a theme that Philip Roth has consistently incorporated in many of his masterpiece novels. Although much of the discussion surrounding identity and Roth focus on select texts such as *The Human Stain* and *The Plot Against America*, Timmothy Parrish notes that the novel *American Pastoral* is essential in the discussion because "Zuckerman's reappearance in *American Pastoral* signals Roth's re-evaluation of the fictional stance toward identity" (Parrish 3). In childhood and throughout development, there are countless influences on identity, but they can be divided into two overarching categories: nature and nurture. *American Pastoral* revolves around the relationship between Seymour "the Swede" Levov and his daughter Merry. Most of the debate about *American Pastoral* has focused on the role of consumerism in Merry and the Swede's conflict, yet as this essay will demonstrate consumerism is merely another expression of a deeper divide between father and daughter. Merry is empowered by her environment whereas Seymour is controlled by his environment, and these contradictory interpretations of environment cause their conflict.

Analysis of identity in *American Pastoral* has mostly focused on the narrator, Nathan Zuckerman. Timothy Parrish analyzes Seymour's role in the novel as a window into understanding Zuckerman's identity. He argues that "Through Swede, Roth [. . .] subjects Zuckerman to a systematic deconstruction of his assumptions about the making and unmaking of cultural identity" (Parrish 7). Another majorly discussed theme in *American Pastoral* is food and consumption in relation to Seymour's conflict with Merry. Sarah Bylund tackles this question by analyzing differences in their consumption, specifically "the Swede's eager consumption of the assimilated, bourgeoisie lifestyle" versus Merry's exploitation of "the potent link between consumption and autonomy" (1). Bylund demonstrates how Merry and the Swede understand consumption as a tool toward two very different outcomes. Interestingly, Debra Shostak notes that "In Roth's hands [. . .] the Jewish protagonist's relation to food revives the dead metaphor of *assimilation* so that it regains physiological connotations of *digestion and consumption*" (3). Instead, Shostak understands food as a vessel to redefine assimilation in the modern generation. Analysis of these two themes, consumerism and identity, demonstrate that both stem from Seymour and Merry's relationship with the environment around them; therefore, their conflict is due to their interpretations of environment, not just their different consumerism.

In Roth's novel *American Pastoral*, Merry Levov and Seymour's narratives of childhood mirror one another, both narrated from Nathan Zuckerman's perspective. The novel begins with a Zuckerman's recollections of his childhood idol Seymour Levov, also known by his nickname the Swede. Zuckerman later learns of Seymour's recent death from others gathered at Zuckerman's 45th high school reunion, where he also learns of Seymour's radical activist daughter Merry, who among other things protested the Vietnam War by bombing a general store post office. After learning this information, Zuckerman begins a fictional retelling of Merry's life from Seymour's perspective, informed by his own knowledge of Seymour. The original retelling of Seymour's childhood from Zuckerman's perspective mirrors the later fictional retelling of Merry's childhood because they are both told from Zuckerman's perspective. With both of their childhoods lined up, it is clear where and why their identities differ as each grows.

In his childhood, the Jewish community of Weequahic surrounds Seymour and plays an active role in his life: Seymour remains passive, molded by his environment. The most notable environmental influence is his nickname, the Swede, originally given because his blonde hair and blue eyes make him look remarkably similar to a Swedish child. In his retelling of the beginnings of this nickname, Zuckerman notes that

> As long as Weequahic remained the old Jewish Weequahic [. . .] Doc Ward was known as the guy who'd christened Swede Levov [. . .] A name that made him mythic…not only during his school years but to his schoolmates, in memory, for the rest of their days. (Roth 207–8)

The explanation cannot proceed without reference to the enviroment, the "old Jewish Weequahic," demonstrating that his name, representing his identity, depends upon his surroundings. Furthermore, the structure of the sentences demonstrates Seymour's passivity when influenced by his environment. Seymour is always the object of the verb, controlled by someone or something else. For example, "Doc ward [. . .] christened Swede Levov." Seymour is not only given his name by someone else, showing that someone in his environment is molding his identity, but Seymour is completely passive in the sentence because he is "christened." Even the nickname controls Seymour because it was "a name that made him mythic." Here the name, representing the environment forced on him, molds Seymour and renders him passive. Roth clearly demonstrates that the active role during Seymour's young years is his environment, either directly from the community or by the continual reinforcement of his nickname and the related pressure it carries to conform to that identity. The overpowering effect of this nickname defines his peers' memory of him "for the rest of their days." This clearly demonstrates what Zuckerman means when he says that Seymour became "history's plaything" (Roth 87).

Merry's upbringing demonstrates a radically different interplay between environment, self, and identity in that Merry actively engages her environment. While arguing with her father and grandfather about her radical tactics in combating the Vietnam War, her grandfather says, "You don't have to go around getting angry with your family. You can write letters. You can vote. You can get up on a soapbox and make a speech" (Roth 289). Here, Roth's syntax attributes the deciding factor in Merry's political identity to herself, a personal choice. In this string of four short sentences all sharply starting with "you can" or "you don't have to," Merry has the power to decide on her actions and identity because she becomes the subject of the verb, instead of becoming a controlled object like her father at the same age. Furthermore, her grandfather later describes Merry's political stubbornness saying, "Something is *haywire* with that child" (Roth 291). The emphasis placed on the word "haywire" by the italics identifies Merry's behavior as innate and independent of her environment. "Haywire" refers to a faulty wiring of her brain causing her to act erratically. This innate, biological aspect of her identity takes precedent over the external pressures she feels from her family to conform to a different identity.

Merry's relationship with food further demonstrates her independence from environment's influence. Bylud also tracks Merry's interaction with food, however, she attributes Merry's expression of independence as defiance. At the remarkable age of ten, Merry offers to cook dinner once a week, which Zuckerman notes is motivated because "that way she could be sure that one night a week they got baked ziti"(Roth 228). Bylud attributes this to Merry trying to "undercut her mother's parental jurisdiction" (Bylud 17); however, Merry is simply ensuring that she has influence on her environment. This exact motivation also appears in her behavior with school lunches. Bylud observes that Merry responds to her mother's packed lunches by "discarding or trading away almost everything in those lunches" (Bylud 17). However, the key aspect of Merry's behavior is that she consistently choses to keep only the dime from her lunch bag which she uses to buy ice cream. Therefore, Merry is not defiant because she does not throw away everything that her mother packs for her. Merry choses to keep the one part of her lunch that isn't predetermined, one that she can still control. To Merry, that dime represents the ability to determine her own dietary decisions, similar to her decision to cook at home. The issue is not in the type of food she gets because Merry's mother tries gives her many different options that most kids would love such as "Baloney on white . . . Liverwurst . . . [and] Tuna" (Roth 226–7). Merry, however, rejects them all except for the dime. This trend continues into her adolescence when Merry eats "almost nothing she was served at home" (Roth 100) and instead eats out with her friends. The key to her decision lies in her environment. She only refuses the food served "at home" because it represents a lack of choice and environmental influence that Merry would succumb to by eating it. Merry maintains her active role by being decisive about what she eats.

After the bombing, while living on the run, Merry continues to use food as empowerment. She first uses her cravings for a BLT and vanilla milkshake to re-empower herself. When she feels the urge to call home, she instead decides to order a BLT and vanilla shake because "grinding patiently away with her jaws and her teeth, thoughtfully pulverizing every mouthful into a silage to settle her down [. . .] gave her the courage to go on alone" (Roth 258). It is not the physical meal that empowers Merry, but her thoughtful consumption that gives "her the courage to go on alone." This is emphasized by the description of her consumption, highlighting "her jaws and her teeth" to show that she is taking the active role. Although Bylund lets these mentions of dietary control pass without mention, Merry further uses food to empower herself on her mission by working "in the kitchen of a dive [. . .] to earn money to get to Oregon" (Roth 258) and later by living in a commune where "they grew a lot of their

own food" (Roth 259). Merry actively engages in the very process of growing her food, and consistently maintains and uses her control over her food to keep living in exile.

In her final dietary move, converting to Jainism, Merry solidifies her independence. Her new tenets of life are as follows

> I renounce all killing of living beings, whether subtle or gross, whether movable or immovable.

> I renounce all vices of lying speech arising from anger, or greed, or fear, or mirth.

> I renounce all taking of anything not given, either in a village, or a town, or a wood, either of little or much, or small or great, or living or lifeless things.

> I renounce all sexual pleasures, either with gods, or men, or animals.

> I renounce all attachments, whether little or much, small or great, living or lifeless; neither shall I myself form such attachments, nor cause others to do so, nor consent to their doing so. (Roth 239)

Merry is once again active in her actions. Every sentence begins with "I renounce" asserting herself as the active player. Merry's conversion is inherently related to her food consumption because as a Jain, she only consumes "plant life" (Roth 243). Here Bylud agrees saying "Thus, even Merry's decision to eat only a small amount of plant life empowers her" (Bylud 22). Merry's consumption clearly demonstrate her constant role as the active player in her culinary environment.

Seymour is unable to understand Merry's yearning for control over her environment and therefore he clashes with Merry when he does not understand her motives. From the very beginning of their relationship Merry and Seymour are clearly disconnected in their understanding of each other. For example, Seymour attributes Merry's radical behavior to her environment growing up, specifically the moment she hears the news of a Buddhist monks' self-immolation in Vietnam, but in reality Merry is not violent because of the violence she sees, but because what self-immolation represents. While Gurumurthy Neelakantan understands the effect of seeing these scenes as "imping[ing] on her subconscious as an emblem of the hypnotic power of self-destruct" (Neelakantan 5), I propose that she is shocked because, to Merry, self-immolation represents the last stand for someone who cannot influence their environment. Merry wonders, "Do you have to m-m-melt yourself down in fire to bring p-p-people to their senses?" (Roth154). She is not contemplating destruction as a tool, but instead is baffled that these people have no other means of influencing their environment. The Buddhist monks have no other way of challenging their political leaders and must resort to destroying themselves. To Merry, there is no greater last-resort that self-immolation, so she is motivated to help these people regain influence over their surroundings. Seymour, however, understands the scene differently, saying, "If their set [that is, the Lebovs' television set] had happened to be tuned into another channel or turned off or broken [. . .] Merry would never have seen what she shouldn't have seen and would never have done what she shouldn't have done" (Roth 154). Seymour thinks that Merry is completely molded by her environment, to the point that seeing the self-immolations has so much influence over her that it causes her to turn into an activist. Merry, however, would have eventually faced the situation in Vietnam and, because of her understanding of one's relationship to his or her environment, she would have interpreted the injustices in Vietnam in a similar fashion. She would have seen the oppressed people as having been robbed of their control of their environment and therefore would have felt the same empathy as she felt toward the Buddhist monks.

In her adolescence, Merry and Seymour come into fresh conflict because they have contrasting interpretations of environmental influence. When Merry begins traveling into New York City to live among fellow radical anti-war protesters, Seymour is only worried about the environment she is putting herself into. Seymour understands the environmental influence to be the ultimate factor in shaping Merry, so he is worried when she begins occupying an environment in New York that he does not know. He constantly asks her questions: "Who are they? [. . .]What do they do for a living? How old are they? [. . .]Where do they live? [. . .] How many people stay in this apartment?" (Roth 106). Seymour desperately assails his daughter with questions this way because he wants to understand the environment she wants to join. He questions her on every aspect of this foreign environment, from "who they are" to "where [. . .] they live" and even "how many people stay in [the] apartment." Merry does not understand why her father is so obsessed with the environment she will inhabit because to her, the environment is not an influence. This fundamental misunderstanding between father and daughter breeds conflict and leads them to have the same conversation 67 times (Roth 112), demonstrating that they cannot understand each other's arguments. Their different interpretations of environment cause their conflict. Ultimately, in their last conversation, Merry listens to her father's plea to "continue her activism in Old Rimrock" and "promptly bombs the post office" (Neelakantan 5). In this culminating act of terrorism, Merry definitively demonstrates that her understanding of her father's plea to "Start in your home town Merry" (Roth 113) is to bomb the general store. In their conversation she directly asks, "What am I going to do, march around the general store?" (Roth 112) and Seymour responds by saying, "Bring the war home" (Roth 112). They fundamentally misunderstand each other, and therefore conflict arises between them. In her final act, Merry continues to actively influence her environment by bombing the general store, destroying the building representative of the environment of her hometown, effectively listening to her understanding of her father's advice to "bring the war home."

Analysis of Seymour and Merry's relationship with their environments exposes the tragic flaw in their father-daughter relationship. Their drastically conflicting understanding of environmental influence acts as a barrier in their conversations because they both assume their own understanding of environmental influence is universally accepted. Therefore it is as if they are speaking different languages, doomed to never be able to properly communicate with one another. The one time that Merry listens to her father by bombing the general store, it is the fundamental break in their relationship. Tragically neither Merry nor Seymour understands this fundamental difference, so their originally serene father-daughter relationship was destined to end with a in a destructive disbanding.

Works Cited

Bylund, Sarah. "Merry Levov's BLT Crusade: Food-Fueled Revolt in Roth's American Pastoral." *Philip Roth Studies* 6.1 (2010): 13–30. Print.

Neelakantan, Gurumurthy. "Monster in Newark: Philip Roth's Apocalypse in American Pastoral". *Studies in American Jewish Literature (1981-)*, Vol. 23. Philip Roth's America: The Later Novels (2004), pp. 55–66. (Penn State University Press). Print.

Parrish, Timmothy. "The End of Identity: Philip Roth's American Pastoral." *Shofar: An Interdisciplinary Journal of Jewish Studies* 19.1. (2000): 84-99. Print.

Shostak, Debra. "An Appetite For America: Philip Roth's Antipastorals." *Eating in Eden: Food & American Utopias.* 74–88. (Lincoln, NE: U of Nebraska P), 2006. Print.

Original Assignment—Research

Course: Philip Roth's Early Complaints
Instructor: Orah Minder

Assignment: Write an 8–10 page research paper (double-spaced, 1" margins, 12-point font) that contributes to a scholarly conversation about a theme or image in the Roth text you have chosen. You may compare how a certain theme or image manifests in an earlier work [*Goodbye, Columbus* and/or *Portnoy's Complaint*] to how that image manifests in your research book; but the argument of your paper should focus on how the theme or image manifests in the text you have read for your research essay. You must thoroughly engage with **at least four** scholarly articles in your research essay.

Goals: A successful research essay will use the following skills also used in the close reading assignment and the lens essay assignment:

- Use close readings of primary and secondary texts

- Use secondary sources as lenses through which to view primary texts

- Use effective and sophisticated essay structure

A successful research essay will also demonstrate mastery of the following skills:

- Locating and mastering relevant scholarly articles

- Integrating such articles to help develop your unique argument

- Citing texts with MLA format

The Writer's Process—Daniel Leon

For Daniel Leon, much of the work of his research process came in deciding how to respond in specific to a task considerably more open-ended than the other assignments in his academic experience. "Nick [Van Kley, Daniel's instructor] gave us a lot of freedom in the text we would use," recalls Daniel. "At first, I thought that I would use an older text, but I had already seen *No Country for Old Men* and it was a big film—I saw that there were a lot of directions I could go with it. I wanted to relate the notion that there was a certain group of people the movie sees as being phased out, a certain kind of American of the past." From that initial observation, Daniel worked to develop a research question and a specific project to pursue. Like Benyamin Meschede-Krasa, he narrowed down the possibilities in part by reading the work of other scholars, in his case preliminary research by a fellow member of his writing seminar

> I was reading somebody else's essay that addressed politics regarding a very different set of issues. I thought that it might be interesting to think about, and I started doing a little bit of research. I saw that there was a specific law regarding immigration in the American southwest being debated at the time the film was being made. I decided to address it in general terms while reading the film. I did a lot of research about that law. At first, I focused very specifically on the resolution. It wasn't working exactly, and so I thought more broadly about immigration at the time the film was made. For a lot of these issues, I went to the library looking for a specific book, but then saw a lot of related books shelved right next to it. I found a lot of sources that way.

Through this series of related steps, Daniel successfully narrowed the field and expanded his knowledge of the very large field of immigration issues in the United States. Daniel's movement toward and then back away from a specific immigration law gave him useful knowledge of a specific issue and allowed him to think creatively about other avenues to pursue in further research. Nick Van Kley concurs: "Productive research questions rarely spring forth fully formed. Only after we learn something about the material we're studying do we begin to understand what a good question might look like." From that point, further review of his argument and collaboration with colleagues in the course and his instructor further refined his project into a particular, strongly motivated argument

> Conferencing was helpful. Originally, I had just treated Anton as though he were Mexican, and it would have been a very white-vs-Mexican debate. But Nick focused his attention on the detail that we don't really know what race he is. That sent me in the direction of thinking about the film presenting a white-vs-Other model, and that really got the essay going.

Nick's recollection of Daniel's revision process reveals the full extent of Daniel's willingness to expand his inquiry and revisit his claims

> Of course, the research Daniel performed after his initial draft, and the close-reading insights he refined and extended late in revision contribute as much to the success of the essay as that initial idea does. We met 3 times, and each time he came to the office, I was surprised by how much work he had performed on the piece. His willingness to extend his work independently was impressive; on his own, he extended his research, refined his local claims, and reworked his essay structure. But at the same time, he was always willing to discard or revise the material that his independent work produced. I'm certain his conversations with his peers and with me led to significant changes in the essay, but the conversations he had were only possible because he had invested so much energy beforehand in thinking, researching, and drafting.

Motive remained a significant concept for Daniel in his work to develop and refine his argument. From early in the project, Daniel kept a clear sense of what relevance his specific argument has for broader understandings of American history, or even the importance of thinking critically about unexamined assumptions

> I think a lot of people in America have a lot of stereotypes at work in their thinking, built into the way they act and live without even thinking about it. *No Country for Old Men*, for example—you can't really call it a racist movie or anything like that, but at the same time I tried to demonstrate that you can still be biased in your depiction of the world. People really need to let go of stereotypes, and you have to make sure that your ideas are accurate even when you don't think about how they might hold that certain bias.

In summarizing his process with drafting and revision, Daniel says the following

> Working down to getting a specific thesis, especially as it related to research is a valuable skill. I think I had pretty good theses right away for my other essays, but it's a lot harder in research to work out a specific and a useful thesis. It's very important to get the right analysis by working a lot more. You can have an extremely broad essay with a small amount of analysis elsewhere, but the university demands a much more specific and complete thesis with a lot of analysis to serve it. You need a really specific thesis or you're not going to do very well.

We hope that you find the results of Daniel's work at narrowing his project engaging and rewarding. Daniel demonstrates the rewards that come with working inward from a large field toward a particular and strongly motivated claim within research. Though the field is often larger than other projects, the work of narrowing it can provide the most rewarding of arguments.

How to Create an Inclusive "American Culture": *No Country for Old Men*

Daniel Leon

In the mid 1960's, a sub-genre emerged within the genre of Westerns called "revisionist westerns," interested in "suggesting that the idealist assumptions of the traditional Western formula were naïve and masked the racism, violence, and greed of the historical conquest of the west" (Western Literature Association 1272). Prior to the 1960's, the vast majority of Westerns depicted the relationship between whites and Native Americans as one where natives were stereotypically depicted either as the "bad" enemy of white civilization or the "good" helper of white civilization. (Derounian-Stodola and Levenier 52). In these situations, natives were never seen as part of "American culture." These narratives glorified the violence and "otherness" seen in natives to the point that natives were seen as a lower class of human beings. In revisionist westerns, there is emphasis on depicting the humanistic values of natives and showing the violence caused by poor race relations as tragic instead of glorious. In certain movies, natives were given a more inclusive role in the history and culture of Americans. A good place to examine the role of revisionist western concepts is the 2007 movie, *No Country for Old Men*. While at first glance *No Country for Old Men* may seem like it an odd choice to examine the role of revisionist concepts in the western genre, it fits in surprisingly well with the this genre, particularly with the "Cowboy vs. Indian" subgenre within it. The basic archetype of the "Cowboy vs. Indian" film is that there is a battle between cowboys and Indians usually set in the western part of the United States in the second half of the 19th Century. If the battle between Llewelyn, (debatably) the protagonist of the film, and Anton, the antagonist of the film is seen to be similar to this battle between Cowboys and Indians, and backdrop of the West (much of which has not changed since the 19th century) is considered, the movie fits in well with the western genre and therefore it is appropriate to examine the role of revisionist concepts in it.

The main plotline of the movie *No Country for Old Men* depicts the battle between Llewelyn Moss, a trailer-park living Vietnam War veteran, and the serial killer after him, Anton Chigurh. The movie starts out with Llewelyn finding $2,000,000 from a failed drug deal across the Mexican border that left all the participants dead. After Llewelyn and his wife separate and he becomes a fugitive because he is a suspect in the drug/murder case, he realizes that his real problem is not the police but the psychotic hitman Anton Chigurh, who will stop at nothing to get the money. Through the course of the movie, Chigurh ends up killing both Llewelyn and his wife without legal consequences. The movie organizes itself around the old sheriff's (the inspiration for "old men" in the title of the film) view of events in town as they unfold. In this film, there is a distinction between those characters who fit in with an "American Culture" created by the film and those who don't. The ones who fit in with this "American Culture" tend to be white and display characteristics that appeal to the viewer. The ones who do not fit in with this "American Culture" tend to be Hispanic and are more foreign to the viewer. When thinking about the role of revisionist concepts in this film, particularly the concept of inclusiveness of non-whites in this culture, one may wonder if the film presents a distorted view of what it means to be "American" by giving certain positive qualities to characters who tend to be native to America and are white, and giving more negative qualities to characters who tend to be non-native and are Hispanic.

Although *No Country for Old Men* is still a revisionist western and is by no means intentionally racist, in light of the national debate on immigration which was in full swing at the time of the creation of the film, it can be seen that *No Country for Old Men* promotes a distorted American culture.

At the time at which both Cormac McCarthy's novel *No Country for Old Men* was written (2005) and its film version was produced (2007), the topic of immigration was a largely debated subject among many Americans. At the root of the debate were questions about the rate of immigration into the United States, whether current rates of Hispanic immigration should slow, and of whether stronger efforts should be made to deport immigrants who had earlier entered the United States illegally. As with any debate, many Americans responded to these questions in a polarized manner, with some saying that the U.S. should keep things as they were while others favored a more vigorous response to both legal and illegal border crossings. In many respects, these disagreements boil down to a cultural difference. A main difference between many opponents of immigration and supporters of immigration consists in their conception of "American Culture." In her 2008 book *The New Nativism*, Robin Dale Jacobson explains that a main fear of many Americans, especially those who live in areas of high immigration from Latin-American countries, is that "American Culture" will be destroyed by the surge in immigrants who do not hold "American cultural values" (Jacobson 90). For example, when interviewing respondents about Proposition 187 in California—an act that took away social services from illegal immigrants in the 1990's—one respondent said of Mexicans that "They don't want to assimilate, they don't want to learn our language, they don't want to become citizens because they don't want to fight for this country; they've already made that statement" (Jacobson 97). What "American Culture" means to opponents of immigration is a topic that would take a book to define, but in terms of the context of this essay is an unchanging, predominantly white culture that is considered to be good. In terms of the debate on immigration, this is where many supporters of immigration disagree. It is important to remember that culture is something that is perceived. Many supporters see "American Culture" as a changing culture that is not just defined by white people. Supporters see immigration as a positive way to help Mexicans get better economic opportunities. This view is captured in Amitai Etzioni's essay "Hispanic and Asian Immigrants—America's Last Hope," in which she explains that American society remains in flux, constantly changing depending on factors like immigration. She goes on to say, "I am not suggesting that historically every change to American institutions has been in line with America's core values but that alterations can be made to these institutions and to the core values without undermining them" (Swain 204). This essay will explore the creation and distortion of "American Culture" through consideration of the way in which *No Country for Old Men* creates an "American Culture" that excludes Hispanics, thereby supporting contemporary opposition of immigration. An examination of the three main characters of the book, Llewlyn Moss, Anton Chigurh, and Sheriff Ed Tom Bell, demonstrates this point.

From evidence in the movie, we can see that protagonist Llewelyn Moss, who is white, has many positive stereotypical characteristics that make him an exemplar of "American Culture." On first glance, it may appear that Llewelyn is an odd choice for an idealized character given that he is a Vietnam War Veteran in his mid-30's. Although this may be the case, we must compare this figure to the "Anglo-Saxon Hero" in other films of the Western Genre. Kathryn Derounian-Stodola and James A. Levernier present the idea in *The Indian Captivity Narratives 1550–1900* that "Freudian perspectives, when applied to the captivity narrative, also explain its popularity-at least in part-as an essential fantasy literature reflecting the white male's subconscious ambivalence when confronted by the wilderness" (Derounian-Stodola and Levernier 43). Llewelyn fits this Anglo-Saxon fantasy image very well. First, throughout the movie he is always wearing rugged dirty clothes and he is covered is scars. Just from this image alone, he fits the description of a rugged Wildman. This image continues through the events Llewelyn is portrayed in. One scene that stands out in portraying him as a man of the wilderness is the first chase scene that he is in. After bravely going back to the scene of the drug-murder case to give water to one of the dying men, he is chased by the police in the dark where he outruns a brigade of police cars, is run into a lake where he swims away from bullets, shoots the police dog in the face, and shrugs off his wounds as he becomes a fugitive. Moss epitomizes a man of the wilderness.

While having a white character as an ideal does not exclude minorities from "American Culture" by itself, the choice to have the antagonist Anton Chigurh as the only non-white main character is a discreet example of the creation of an "American Culture" that is defined by the "whiteness" of its citizens. Chigurh is not necessarily Hispanic. He has an Eastern European last name, is played by an actor whose first language is Spanish, and appears nonwhite in comparison to Moss. Throughout the film, Anton behaves in consistently cruel, sadistic, and self-interested ways. From his looks, he is tall, muscular, and has an intimidating face, to say nothing of the fact that he regularly commits murders with a device used to kill cows in a slaughterhouse. The epitome of his evilness can be seen in the scene in which he terrorizes an elderly cashier. This occurs when Anton goes into a gas station to pay for his gas and he intimidates the jolly cashier into playing a game of coin toss with him. The cashier's jolly

attitude soon turns to one of pure fear when Anton repeatedly asks, "What is the most you ever lost in a coin toss?" Because the film has already shown Anton murder others, the viewer may wonder whether or not Anton will kill the man. After a long, intimidating "game" of coin toss, Anton walks out, giving the cashier and the viewer sense of relief balanced against a better understanding of the danger and horror Anton represents. In this, the negative connotations of Anton's "otherness" amplify the "otherness" already associated with the Hispanic minority in Western movies. At the same time, this amplifies the greatness of the white man by piling all of the film's danger onto a nonwhite character, thereby making the connection between "American Culture" and "White Culture" even stronger.

While the context in which both Llewelyn and Anton are placed can promote an association between "American Culture" and "White Culture," the content of Sheriff Bell's character likewise promotes this association. This is most prominently exemplified in the scene in which the Sheriff calls Clara Jean to tell her that he wants to help Llewelyn. In this scene, the Sheriff goes out of his way to make a genuine offer to Clara Jean, Llewelyn's wife, to help protect Llewelyn from Anton. The sheriff promises Clara Jean that he will make sure not to get Llewelyn in trouble. By doing this he breaks the law because at this point in the movie Llewelyn is a fugitive and prime suspect in a drug/murder case. While this is a nice deed, it is also clearly discriminatory given how he treats Chigurh the other, nonwhite fugitive. First of all, Llewelyn is suspected of killing about a dozen people. Although the movie viewer knows this to be false, the sheriff has no clue that this is so. Given this, Llewelyn has potentially from the sheriff's point of view killed more people than Anton. The act of calling Clara Jean might be justified if the sheriff had a special relationship with Llewelyn or was generally a very kind person, yet he demonstrates neither characteristic. From the evidence seen in the movie, the sheriff has no real relationship with Llewelyn and in most ways seems cold, distant, and cynical. In fact, after seeing dead Hispanics from the same drug deal that makes Llewelyn a fugitive he shows no sympathy and even laughs! From the evidence just given, the differences in the way the sheriff treats Llewelyn and the way he treats Anton can only come down to race, a difference in behavior the film endorses and treats as reasonable. This discrimination by a figure of authority, whom the movie treats as legitimate and respectable, works to create this particular white "American Culture."

In addition to this, the sheriff's opening monologue and the imagery presented with it in the beginning of *No Country for Old Men*, expresses nostalgia, which the film uses as a tool to reinforce "American Culture." The sheriff opens *No Country for Old Men* by saying, "I was sheriff of this county when I was 25 years old. Hard to believe. My grandfather was a lawman. Father too. Me and him was sheriffs at the same time, him up in Plano and me out here. I think he's pretty proud of that. I know I was." The sheriff's words create a clear sense of nostalgia as he reflects upon his long-passed younger days. The sheriff enhances this sense of nostalgia through the slow, deliberate way in which the sheriff says each sentence, pausing as the camera provides a vision of desolate desert scenery. As the sheriff narrates his words, the viewer is shown images of the desert at sunrise. The sheriff's lone narration over this large desert conveys a sense of gravity and deep meaning. The desert is an empty place devoid of life and activity implying an earlier time of life and growth, and the sheriff's narration as the sun rises is a symbol for his loneliness: the sheriff is the lonely man in a place that once was. This is even further enhanced by the fact that, presumably, the only thing that the viewer knows about the movie at this point is that its title is *No Country for Old Men*. This title, which strongly correlates to the image of a "lonely man in a place that once was," is a nostalgic title given by its meaning that as men become old there is no place for them. The combination of knowing the title and looking at the sheriff establishes a strong tone of nostalgia within the first few seconds of the movie. Having nostalgia does not necessarily establish anything by itself, but when it is put in context of a personality and movie that contains many elements of building an "American Culture" without immigrants, this portrayal of nostalgia may cause viewers to mourn for this sense of "American Culture" created in the movie. Therefore it reinforces that "American Culture" created at other points in the movie.

Although the film by itself is just a movie, creating this sense of nostalgia can contribute to the creation of a cultural environment damaging to the lives of many people. An example of this technique appears in Kent A. Ono and John M. Sloop's 2002 book *Shifting Border: Rhetoric, Immigration, and California's Proposition 187*. In this book the authors look at many Californian newspapers' reactions toward Proposition 187 and try to find trends. A particularly interesting trend appears in the many newspaper articles that associate crime with immigration. As Ono and Sloop say, "news discourse constructs undocumented workers as criminals either because they are prone to take part in illegal activities such as gang violence if they are not let into school or cannot find employment" (28). This view also appears in Robin Jacobson's *The New Nativism* where in her survey numerous respondents likewise connected immigrants and crime. Yet, to what extent is this true? Graham C. Ousey and Charles E. Kubrin's 2009 article "Exploring the Connection between Immigration and Violent Crime Rates in U.S. Cities, 1980-2000" explains how the popular conception linking immigration and crime rates departs from reality. He proves that far deeper issues determine what happens to crime rates when immigrants arrive. For example, he says that there is no sufficient evidence to prove that Latinos are particularly involved in the drug trade (and that this myth is reinforced by popular Hollywood blockbusters!) (Ousey and Kubrin 450). Joel Millman's 1997 book *The Other Americans* makes a similar claim about immigration, arguing that the reason for the drastic drop in crime in New York in the 1990s was because of immigrants. He demonstrates that during the time crime dropped in New York City, immigration rates tripled. If this is true, how can authors of California's newspapers and respondents to surveys claim such a connection between immigration and crime? The primary reason for this is a sense of nostalgia that does not match up with the reality of the past. People remember a past in which there was less crime and less immigrants but the two do not necessarily have any connection. This same mechanism informs the nostalgia of *No Country for Old Men*, which risks constructing a false sense of the past.

Toward the end of the movie, a hope emerges that the film may replace the sheriff's nostalgia with a more realistic perspective, the sheriff's father enters the narrative. This occurs in the scene where the sheriff meets with his father to tell him that he is retiring. His father, who was the old sheriff of the county, lives in a disordered shack in the middle of the desert and is in a wheelchair. This image is very surprising. From the opening lines, the younger sheriff sounds like the last of a noble breed rather than still living with a father who is shown as the opposite of glorious. We then learn that the older sheriff was forced to leave his position after he was shot and that the younger sheriff's great-uncle was gunned down by Indians at his front porch when he was walking in. This dialogue completely contradicts the earlier image of the old days as glorious and larger than life. Nostalgia meets reality more forcefully when Llewelyn asks his father what he would do, hypothetically speaking, if the person who shot him, who in reality died in jail in another example of "the good old days," was pardoned. The elder sheriff answers this by saying "Nothing. Wouldn't be no point in it...all the time ya spend trying to get back what's been took from ya, more is going out the door. After a while you just have to try to get a tourniquet on it." In this sentence the sheriff suggests looking towards the future instead of wasting time being angry at the past. This could serve as a useful metaphor for immigrants, suggesting that you must move past the days when the country had a different demographic makeup and accept what is here now. At the very least, it replaces mythic nostalgia with the reality of life as it is now.

Yet the sheriff's father undermines this more realistic approach to America with a single monologue. After talking about how his uncle was gunned down on his own porch, the sheriff's father looks at his son, who seriously considers quitting his job as sheriff because he feels "overmatched" by his situation with Llewelyn and Anton. The father looks his son in the eye and says, "What you got ain't nothing new. This country's hard on people, you can't stop what's coming. They ain't all waiting on you. That's vanity." The father's tone of voice gives this scene added gravity. Before, when the sheriff's father talks about his past, he talks in a somewhat carefree voice only hindered by sadness when talking about the death of his uncle. When he goes to give his son this advice, though, he becomes very serious and intense. This makes his monologue a dire warning, underlined in its seriousness by the lighter conversation that comes before. That is, by saying that if you don't stop what is going on, i.e. the deterioration of "American Culture," you will end up like me: as the title says, there is no country for old men. By using the phrase "they ain't all waiting on you" he refers specifically to people who are different. In this, he is solidifying two groups of categorization, one group being those of the old culture and the other of the new. The warning culminates at the very end of the scene. As the last word of the sheriff's father rolls off his tongue, a new scene begins with a close-up shot of Llewelyn's gravestone. This shot is the first time we learn he had died, implicitly murdered by Chigurh. As the camera slowly rolls down we observe his grave for close to ten seconds. During these ten seconds, the viewer is forced to think about Llewlyn's death and what it means. This image of a gravestone right after he speaks is the ultimate warning sign of what will happen if outsiders continue to infiltrate and change "American Culture."

It is clear that *No Country for Old Men* presents a distorted "American Culture" in which native-born whites are given an elevated status. Given the national debate on immigration at the time of this movie, it has no doubt been informed by and has perhaps in turn informed the debate surrounding immigrants, particularly those who are Hispanic. Since this movie came out in 2007, Congress has hurt immigrants in many ways. According to the *New York Times*, Obama had four years into his presidency deported more immigrants than George Bush did in eight years (Shear 1). Arizona passed SB 1070, a bill that according to the *New York Times* "requires state law enforcement officials to determine the immigration status of anyone they stop or arrest if they have reason to suspect that the individual might be in the country illegally" (Liptak A1). What is scary about this Arizona law, in terms of what was discussed in this essay, is that officers have the right to determine if someone looks like an illegal immigrant. Yet how can someone "look like they are an illegal immigrant"? To no surprise, this can only be achieved by racial profiling, profiling based off of whom Americans see to not fit in. This type of profiling, even when successful in reducing crime, leads to the creation of false identities of who belongs and who does not. In *No Country for Old Men*, (from the point of the law) both Anton and Llewelyn were highly dangerous criminals, yet only Llewelyn, the character who "fit in" with American Culture, was helped by the Sheriff. Was the sheriff profiling Anton because he is different? There is hope, though. As Hispanics and immigrants in general continue to make a presence in the U.S., they will likely move on from being on the outskirts of film to the ones who are writing it, and will hopefully be able to create an "American Culture" that excludes nobody.

Works Cited

Derounian-Stodola, Katherine and James Levenier. *The Indian Captivity Narrative 1550–1900*. New York: Twayne Publishers, 1993. Print.

Etzioni, Amatai. "Hispanic and Asian Immigrants: America's Last Hope." Carol M. Swain. New York: Cambridge University Press, 2007. 189–206. Print.

Jacobson, Robin Dale. *The New Nativism*. Minneapolis: University of Minnesota, 2008. Print.

Liptak, Adam. "Blocking Parts of Arizona Law, Justices Allow its Centerpiece." *New York Times*: 25 June 2012:A1. Print.

Michael D. Shear. "Seeing Citizen's Path Near, Activists Push Obama to Slow Deportations." *New York Times*. 22 February 2013: A12. Print.

Miller, Joel. *The Other Americans*. New York: Viking. 1997. Print

No Country For Old Men. Dir. Ethan Coen and Joel Coen. Perf. Tommy Lee Jones, Javier Bardem, Josh Brolin. Paramount Vantage, 2007. DVD.

Ono, Kent A. and John M. Sloop. *Shifting Borders: Rhetoric, Immigration, and California's Proposition 187*. Philadelphia: Temple University Press, 2002. Print.

Ousey, Graham C. and Charis E. Kurbin. "Exploring the Connection between Immigration and Violent Crime Rates in U.S. Cities, 1980–2000." *Social Problems* Vol. 56, No. 3 (August 2009). 447–473. Web. 11 Dec. 2013.

Western Literature Association. *A Literary History of the American West*. Fort Worth: Texas Christian University Press, 1987. Print.

Original Assignment—Research

Course: The New Old West
Instructor: Nick Van Kley

For this assignment you will perform research and write a 10-12 page essay (not including the required Works Cited page). The essay should interpret a relatively contemporary text, figure, or event of your choosing. Your field of inquiry should deal with current representations of or conversations about the American West. You can find a list of potential subjects on our LATTE page. In order to kick start your analysis of your chosen subject, you should use at least one of the critical texts that we read in this unit. As always, your paper should have a unified thesis, a genuine motive, offer compelling evidence, and pursue a developmental structure. You should think of your project as having three categories of sources:

The Primary Text(s)

You should limit yourself to a relatively short primary object of analysis. This might be a full-length film, a few episodes of a TV series, a poem, a speech, a handful of records from a relatively limited historical event, a series of interviews you perform, a government report, or a host of other "texts." Feel free to pursue your own interests and to be creative. Remember, however, that this assignment requires close reading (i.e. the careful examination of concrete detail) just as the others did. Don't find yourself with too much material and not enough analysis. You should also be sure that you can say something about the way the text or texts go about representing a revision of the tropes of the Old West. If you're having trouble finding a suitable text, visit the LATTE page for a list of suggestions.

The Lens

Choose one or more of the critical texts you read in this unit to help you produce insight about your primary text(s). You are welcome to use the readings that we've discussed in class, but you're also welcome to seek out your own texts that tell you about some aspect of the representation of Westerns. These sources will likely work similarly to the lens text from essay 2. They will give you useful keyterms that you will use to drive your interpretation and to enter into an already existing scholarly conversation. Remember, lens analysis is not just a genre of essay; it is also an analytical move we perform in all kinds of contexts. It is important that this essay avoid merely repeating the ideas from the lens text, however, so while you may use Derounian-Stodola and Levernier's book again in this essay, you must focus on ideas that were not present in your lens essay.

The Research

Once you have an idea of the theoretical framework you'd like to deploy (or the interpretive questions you would like to ask), you must do some further research using the resources available to you through our library. In addition to your primary source(s), you should locate, read, and fully engage with at least 5 secondary sources. At least 3 of these sources should be scholarly, peer-reviewed journal articles or scholarly books. While you can use as many scholarly sources as you like, 3 of these scholarly sources must be sources you have found (i.e., they cannot come from the assigned readings). You might also want to use non-interpretive, factual sources, like interviews or news reports. These are good sources, but they don't count toward the peer-reviewed source requirement.

Remember that your ultimate goal is to enter into an ongoing critical conversation by contributing a new claim. So, your research should help you explain how your claim makes that contribution.

Excerpts from
Writing Analytically

Excerpts from *Writing Analytically*

A Preface

The remainder of this volume contains excerpts from David Rosenwasser and Jill Stephen's writing manual, *Writing Analytically*. The book casts writing as a tool for analytical thinking, and many of the excerpts included here bear the mark of that way of thinking. The stages of producing a compelling analytical argument are also steps we take to build better ideas. Writing analytically, according to Rosenwasser and Stephen, is a great way to become a better thinker.

The excerpts we have chosen to include here offer advice for a host of writing processes:

- "Pushing Observations to Conclusions" offers a technique for locating pieces of evidence that could become the foundations for compelling arguments and pushing our thinking beyond initial responses.

- "Linking Evidence and Claims" reminds us just how important it is to articulate the relationship between the claims we advance and the evidence we use to support them.

- "Moving from Description to Analysis" explains the difference between descriptive and analytical writing and suggests that descriptive writing is a technique we can use to turn our buried assumptions into focused, analytical moves.

- "Making a Thesis Evolve" reminds us that a thesis should not be a static claim; rather, it should evolve through the process of revision, changing to accommodate complicating or anomalous evidence.

- "What to Do with a Reading" and "What to Do with Secondary Sources" detail the utility of bringing secondary voices into our analytical projects and help us consider techniques for making those sources productive for our projects.

- "The Function of Conclusions" proposes that conclusions must do more than merely recount the major ideas of an essay and offers some ideas for concluding effectively.

- "Plagiarism and the Logic of Citation" explains just what constitutes plagiarism and why academic citation practices are vital for our scholarly endeavors.

We offer this material not because it captures the "right" way to think about critical thinking and analytical writing, but because we think it offers a set of useful starting points for conversation. Communities of writers need to build a shared vocabulary in order to communicate effectively about the writing process. These passages might form a foundation for your writerly community's vocabulary, but it's up to you to fill the gaps they leave undressed.

Pushing Observations to Conclusions: Asking So What?

The prompt for making the move from observation to implication and ultimately interpretation is: So what? The question is shorthand for questions such as the following:

Why does this observation matter? What does it mean?
Where does this observation get us?
How can we begin to generalize about the subject?

Asking, So what? is a calling to account, which is why, in conversation, its force is potentially rude. That is, the question intervenes rather peremptorily with a "Why does *this* matter?" It is thus a challenge to make meaning through a creative leap—to move beyond the patterns and emphases you've been observing in the data to tentative conclusions on what these observations suggest.

The peremptoriness of the So what? question can, we think, be liberating. Okay, take the plunge, it says. Start laying out possible interpretations. And, when you are tempted to stop thinking too soon, asking So what? will press you onward.

At the least, consider asking and answering So what? at the ends of paragraphs. And then, if you ask So what? again of the first answer you've offered, you'll often tell yourself where your thinking needs to go next.

For example, let's say you make a number of observations about the nature of e-mail communication—it's cheap, informal, often grammatically incorrect, full of abbreviations ("IMHO"), and ephemeral (impermanent). You rank these and decide that its ephemerality is most interesting. So what? Well, that's why so many people use it, you speculate, because it doesn't last. So what that its popularity follows from its ephemerality? Well, apparently we like being released from the hard-and-fast rules of formal communication; e-mail frees us. So what? Well, . . .

The repeated asking of this question causes people to push on from and pursue the implications of their first responses; it prompts people to reason in a chain, rather than settling prematurely for a single link.

Linking Evidence and Claims

The Function of Evidence

A common assumption about evidence is that it is "the stuff that proves I'm right." Although this way of thinking about evidence is not wrong, it is much too limited. Corroboration (proving the validity of a claim) is one of the functions of evidence, but not the only one.

It helps to remember that the word *prove* actually comes from a Latin verb meaning "to test." The noun form of prove, *proof*, has two meanings: (1) evidence sufficient to establish a thing as true or believable, and (2) the act of testing for truth or believability. When you operate on the first definition of proof alone, you are far more likely to seek out evidence that supports only your point of view, ignoring or dismissing other evidence that could lead to a different and possibly better idea. You might also assume that you can't begin writing until you have arrived at an idea you're convinced is right, since only then could you decide which evidence to include. Both of these practices close down your thinking instead of leading you to a more open process of formulating and testing ideas.

Beginning with the goal of establishing an idea as believable and true can interfere with the need to examine the idea. Moreover, this approach can lead to an unnecessarily combative debate style of argument in which the aim is to win the game and defeat one's opponents. In debate style, convincing others that you're right is more important than arriving at a fair and accurate assessment of your subject. By contrast, the advantage to following the second definition of the word proof—in the sense of testing—is that you will be better able to negotiate among competing points of view. In addition, this practice will predispose your readers to consider what you have to say, because you are offering them not only the thoughts a person has had, but also a person in the act of thinking.

The Fallacy That Facts Can Speak for Themselves

Evidence rarely, if ever, can be left to speak for itself. The word *evident* comes from a Latin verb meaning "to see." To say that the truth of a statement is "self-evident" means that it does not need proving because its truth can be plainly seen by all. When a writer leaves evidence to speak for itself, he or she is assuming that it can be interpreted in only one way, and that readers necessarily will think as the writer does.

But the relationship between evidence and claims is rarely self-evident: that relationship virtually *always* needs to be explained. One of the key analytical moves of Chapter 2 was making the implicit explicit. That is also the rule in the domain of evidence. Perhaps the single most important lesson about using evidence that this chapter has to teach is that the thought connections that have occurred to you will not automatically occur to others. Persuasive writing always makes the connections between evidence and claim overt.

Writers who think that evidence speaks for itself often do very little with their evidence except put it next to their claims: "The party was terrible: there was no alcohol"—or, alternatively, "The party was great: there was no alcohol." Just juxtaposing the evidence with the claim leaves out the thinking that connects them, thereby implying that the logic of the connection is obvious. But even for readers prone to agreeing with a given claim, simply pointing to the evidence is not enough.

It should be acknowledged, however, that the types and amounts of evidence necessary for persuading readers and building authority also vary from one discipline to another, as does the manner in which the evidence is presented. Although some disciplines—the natural sciences, for example—require writers to present evidence first and then interpret it, others (the humanities and some social sciences) expect interpretation of the evidence as it is presented. In all disciplines—and virtually any writing situation—it is important to support claims with evidence, to make evidence lead to claims, and especially to be explicit about how you've arrived at the connection between your evidence and your claims (see Figure 5.1).

Of course, before you can attend to the relationship between evidence and claims, you first have to make sure to include both of them. Let's pause to take a look at how to remedy the problems posed by leaving one out: unsubstantiated claims and pointless evidence.

Supporting Unsubstantiated Claims: Providing Evidence

Problem: Making claims that lack supporting evidence.
Solution: Learn to recognize and support unsubstantiated assertions.

Unsubstantiated claims occur when a writer concentrates only on conclusions, omitting the evidence that led to them. At the opposite extreme, pointless evidence results when a writer offers a mass of detail attached to an overly general claim. Both of these problems can be solved by offering readers the evidence that led to the claim and explaining how the evidence led there. The word *unsubstantiated* means "without substance." An unsubstantiated claim is not necessarily false; it just offers none of the concrete "stuff" upon which the claim is based. When a writer makes an unsubstantiated claim, he or she has assumed that readers will believe it just because the writer put it out there.

Perhaps more important, unsubstantiated claims deprive you of details. As Chapter 1 has argued, without details you're left with nothing concrete to think about. If you lack some actual "stuff" to analyze, you can easily get stuck in a set of abstractions, which tend to overstate your position and leave your readers wondering exactly what you mean. The further away your language gets from the concrete, from references to physical detail—things that you can see, hear, count, taste, smell, and touch—the more abstract it becomes. An aircraft carrier anchored outside a foreign harbor is concrete; the phrase *intervening in the name of democracy* is abstract.

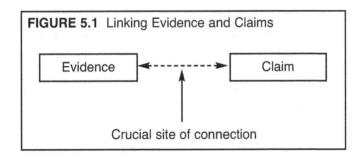

FIGURE 5.1 Linking Evidence and Claims

Evidence ←- - - - - - -→ Claim

Crucial site of connection

Distinguishing Evidence from Claims

To check your drafts for unsubstantiated assertions, you first have to know how to recognize them. A fundamental skill to possess is the ability to *distinguish* evidence from claims. It is sometimes difficult to separate facts from judgments, data from interpretations of the data. Writers who aren't practiced in this skill can believe that they are offering evidence when they are really offering only unsubstantiated claims. In your own reading and writing, pause once in a while to label the sentences of a paragraph as either evidence *(E)* or claims *(C)*. What happens if we try to categorize the sentences of the following paragraph in this way?

> The owners are ruining baseball in America. Although they claim they are losing money, they are really just being greedy. A few years ago, they even fired the commissioner, Fay Vincent, because he took the players' side. Baseball is a sport, not a business, and it is a sad fact that it is being threatened by greedy businessmen.

The first and last sentences of the paragraph are claims. They draw conclusions about as yet unstated evidence that the writer will need to provide. The middle two sentences are harder to classify. If particular owners have said publicly that they are losing money, the existence of the owners' statements is a fact. But the writer moves from evidence to unsubstantiated claims when he suggests that the owners are lying about their financial situation and are doing so because of their greed. Similarly, it is a fact that commissioner Fay Vincent was fired, but only an assertion that he was fired "because he took the players' side." Although many of us might be inclined to accept some version of the writer's claim as true, we should not be asked to accept his opinion as self-evident truth. What is the evidence in support of the claim? What are the reasons for believing that the evidence means what he says it does?

Giving Evidence a Point: Making Details Speak

> **Problem:** Presenting a mass of evidence without explaining how it relates to the claims.
> **Solution:** Make details speak. Explain how evidence confirms and qualifies the claim.

Your thinking emerges in the way that you follow through on the implications of the evidence you have selected. You need to interpret it for your readers. You have to make the details speak, conveying to your readers *why* they mean what you claim they mean.

The following example illustrates what happens when a writer leaves the evidence to speak for itself.

> Baseball is a sport, not a business, and it is a sad fact that it is being threatened by greedy businessmen. For example, Eli Jacobs, the previous owner of the Baltimore Orioles, recently sold the team to Peter Angelos for one hundred million dollars more than he had spent ten years earlier when he purchased it. Also, a new generation of baseball stadiums have been built in the last decade—in Baltimore, Chicago, Arlington (Texas), Cleveland, and most recently, in San Francisco, Milwaukee, Houston, and Philadelphia. These parks are enormously expensive and include elaborate scoreboards and luxury boxes. The average baseball players, meanwhile, now earn more than a million dollars a year, and they all have agents to represent them. Alex Rodriguez, the shortstop for the New York Yankees, is paid more than twenty million dollars a season. Sure, he set a record for most homers in a season by a shortstop, but is any ballplayer worth that much money?

Unlike the previous example, which was virtually all claims, this paragraph, except for the opening claim and the closing question, is all evidence. The paragraph presents what we might call an "evidence sandwich": it encloses a series of facts between two claims. (The opening statement blames "greedy businessmen," presumably owners, and the closing statement appears to indict greedy, or at least overpaid, players.) Readers are left with two problems. First, the mismatch between the opening and concluding claims leaves it not altogether clear what the writer is saying that the evidence suggests. And second, he has not told readers why they should believe that the evidence means what he says it does. Instead, he leaves it to speak for itself.

If readers are to accept the writer's implicit claims—that the spending is too much and that it is ruining baseball—he will have to show *how* and *why* the evidence supports these conclusions. The rule that applies here is that *evidence can almost always be interpreted in more than one way.*

We might, for instance, formulate at least three conclusions from the evidence offered in the baseball paragraph. We might decide that the writer believes baseball will be ruined by going broke or that its spirit will be ruined by becoming too commercial. Worst of all, we might disagree with his claim and conclude that baseball is not really being ruined, since the evidence could be read as signs of health rather than decay. The profitable resale of the Orioles, the expensive new ballparks (which, the writer neglects to mention, have drawn record crowds), and the skyrocketing salaries all could testify to the growing popularity rather than the decline of the sport.

How to Make Details Speak: An Example   The best way to begin making the details speak is to take the time to look at them, asking questions about what they imply.

1. Say explicitly what you take the details to mean.
2. State exactly how the evidence supports your claims.
3. Consider how the evidence complicates (qualifies) your claims.

The writer of the baseball paragraph leaves some of his claims and virtually all of his reasoning about the evidence implicit. What, for example, bothers him about the special luxury seating areas? Attempting to uncover his assumptions, we might speculate that he intends it to demonstrate how economic interests are taking baseball away from its traditional fans because these new seats cost more than the average person can afford. This interpretation could be used to support the writer's governing claim, but *he would need to spell out the connection, to reason back to his own premises.* He might say, for example, that baseball's time-honored role as the all-American sport—democratic and grass-roots—is being displaced by the tendency of baseball as a business to attract higher box office receipts and wealthier fans.

The writer could then make explicit what his whole paragraph implies, that baseball's image as a popular pastime in which all Americans can participate is being tarnished by players and owners alike, whose primary concerns appear to be making money. In making his evidence speak in this way, the writer would be practicing step 3 above—using the evidence to complicate and *refine* his ideas. He would discover which specific aspect of baseball he thinks is being ruined, clarifying that the "greedy businessmen" to whom he refers include both owners and players.

Let's emphasize the final lesson gleaned from this example. When you focus on tightening the links between evidence and claim, the result is almost always a "smaller" claim than the one you set out to prove. This is what evidence characteristically does to a claim: it shrinks and restricts its scope. This process, also known as qualifying a claim, is the means by which a thesis develops (or as we call it in Chapter 6, evolves).

Sometimes it is hard to give up on the large, general assertions that were your first response to your subject. But your sacrifices in scope are exchanged for greater accuracy and validity. The sweeping claims you lose ("Greedy businessmen are ruining baseball") give way to less resounding but also more informed, more incisive, and less judgmental ideas ("Market pressures may not bring the end of baseball, but they are certainly changing the image and nature of the game").

Moving from Description to Interpretation

What is the difference between a description or a summary and analysis? And, at what point does analysis become interpretation? What we have suggested thus far is that analysis implies a search for meaning, and that analysis and interpretation are inseparable. The process of noticing, of recording selected details and patterns of detail (analysis) is already the beginning of interpretation. But, once the move from observation to conclusions begins, writers need to make explicit and defend the appropriateness of the interpretive context in which this leap takes place.

Differentiating Analysis from Summary

Summary differs from analysis, because the aim of summary is to recount—in effect, to reproduce someone else's ideas. But summary and analysis are also clearly related and usually operate together. Summary is important to analysis, since you can't analyze a subject without laying out its significant parts for your reader. Similarly, analysis is important to summary, because summarizing is more than just copying someone else's words. We offer both our description/summary and our analysis of a painting—*Whistler's Mother*—to demonstrate the difference between the two ways of approaching subjects. You will see, however, that our analysis would not be possible without the description that allowed us to see which patterns of detail in the painting to attend to.

Figure 3.1 *Arrangement in Grey and Black: The Artist's Mother by James Abbott McNeill Whistler, 1871.*

How would an analysis of this painting differ from a summary of it?

Try this 3.1: Analyzing *Whistler's Mother*

You will be better able to make use of our analysis of the picture if you try to do your own analysis of it first. Start with the steps of the observational strategy "looking for patterns of repetition and contrast" (the Method). What details repeat in the picture? What patterns of similar detail (strands) can you find? What details and patterns of detail seem to fall into organizing contrasts? Compile your three lists in writing; then rank the top two in each category, and write a paragraph on why you would choose one of these as most important.

A primary aim of this book's observation strategies, as you will recall, is to shift your attention from premature generalizing about a subject to recording detail that actually appears in it. Description is the best antidote to what we call in Chapter 1 the dogfish problem—trying to start with an idea about your subject without first really looking at it. This book's basic formula can be stated as follows:

- **What do you notice?**
- **What repeats?**
- **What is opposed to what?**
- **So what?**

Try applying this formula to the painting.

Summary, like analysis, is a tool of understanding and not just a mechanical task. But a summary stops short of analysis because summary typically makes much smaller interpretive leaps. A summary of the painting popularly known as *Whistler's Mother*, for example, would tell readers what the painting includes, which details are the most prominent, and even what the overall effect of the painting seems to be. A summary might say that the painting possesses a certain serenity, and that it is somewhat spare, almost austere. This kind of language still fills into the category of focused description, which is what a summary is.

An analysis would include more of the writer's interpretive thinking. It might tell us, for instance, that the painter's choice to portray his subject in profile contributes to our sense of her separateness from us and of her nonconfrontational passivity. We look at her, but she does not look back at us. Her black dress and the fitted lace cap that obscures her hair are not only emblems of her *self-effacement*, disguising her identity like her expressionless face, but also the tools of her *self-containment* and thus of her power to remain aloof from prying eyes. What is the attraction of this painting (this being one of the questions that an analysis might ask)? What might draw a viewer to the sight of this austere, drably attired woman, sitting alone in the center of a mostly blank space? Perhaps it is the very starkness of the painting, and the mystery of self-sufficiency at its center, that attracts us. (See Figure 3.1.)

Observations of this sort go beyond describing what the painting contains and enter into the writer's ideas about what its details imply, what the painting invites us to make of it and by what means.

Notice in our analysis of the painting how intertwined the description (summary) is with the analysis. Laying out the data is key to any kind of analysis, not simply because it keeps the analysis accurate but because, crucially, it is in the act of carefully describing a subject that analytical writers often have their best ideas.

You may not agree with the terms by which we have summarized the picture, and thus you may not agree with such conclusions as "the mystery of self-sufficiency." Nor is it necessary that you agree, because *there is no single, right answer to what the painting is about.* The absence of a single right answer does not, however, mean that anything goes.

As we discuss in more detail below (under the heading "The Limits on Interpretation"), your readers' willingness to accept an analytical conclusion is powerfully connected to their ability to see its *plausibility*—that is, how it follows from both the supporting details that you have selected and the language you have used in characterizing those details. The writer who can offer a plausible (not necessarily or obviously true, but believable) description of a subject's key features is likely to arrive at conclusions about possible meanings that others would share. Often the best that you can hope for with analytical conclusions is not that others will say, "Yes, that is obviously right," but "Yes, I can see where it might be possible and reasonable to think as you do."

Figure 3.2 Summary and analysis of *Whistler's Mother* diagram

Data	Method of Analysis	Interpretive Leaps
subject in profile, not looking at us	make implicit explicit (speculate about what the detail might suggest)	figure strikes us as separate, nonconfrontatonal, passive.
folded hands, fitted lace cap, contained hair, expressionless face	locate pattern of same or similar detail; make what is implicit in pattern of details explicit	figure strikes us as self-contained, powerful in her separateness and self-enclosure self-sufficient?
patterned curtain and picture versus still figure and blank wall; slightly frilled lace cuffs and ties on cap versus plain black dress	locate organizing contrast; make what is implicit in the contrast explicit	austerity and containment of the figure made more pronounced by slight contrast with busier, more lively, and more ornate elements and with little picture showing world outside
slightly slouched body position and presence of suppport for feet	anomalies; make what is implicit in the anomalies explicit	These details destabilize the serenity of the figure, adding some tension to the picture in the form of slightly uneasy posture and figure's need for support: she looks too long, drooped in on her own spine.

Summary and Analysis of *Whistler's Mother*

Here are two general rules to be drawn from this discussion of analysis and summary:

1. **Describe with care.** The words you choose to summarize your data will contain the germs of your ideas about what the subject means.

2. **In moving from summary to analysis,** look consciously at the language you have chosen, asking, "Why did I choose this word? What ideas are implicit in the language I have used?"

Differentiating Analysis from Expressive Writing

In expressive writing, your primary subject is yourself, with other subjects serving as a means of evoking greater self-understanding. In analytical writing, your reasoning may derive from personal experience, but it is your reasoning and not you or your experiences that matter. Analysis asks not just the expressive question, "What do I think?" but "How good is my thinking? How well does it fit the subject I am trying to explain?"

We don't mean to suggest that expressive writing cannot be analytical or that analytical writing cannot be expressive. Expressive (writer-centered) writing is analytical in its attempts to define and explain a writer's feelings, reactions, and experiences. And analysis is a form of self-expression, since it inevitably reflects the ways a writer's experiences have taught him or her to think about the world.

Although observations like those offered in the preceding interpretive leaps column go beyond simple description, they don't move from the picture into autobiography. They stay with the task of explaining the painting, rather than moving to private associations that the painting might prompt, such as effusions about old age, or rocking chairs, or the character and situation of the writer's own grandmother. Such associations could well be valuable unto themselves as a means of prompting a searching piece of expressive writing. They might also help a writer interpret some feature of the painting that he or she was working to understand. But the writer would not be free to use pieces of his or her personal history as conclusions about what the painting communicates unless these conclusions could also be reasonably inferred from the painting itself.

Let's say, for example, that a writer believed that the woman is mourning the death of a son or is patiently waiting to die. In support of these theories, the writer might cite the black dress, the woman's somber expression, and the relative darkness of the painting. This selection of details might be sufficient to support some kind of interpretation concerning sadness or loss, but would clearly not support a leap to an implied narrative about a dead son. To make such a leap would be to substitute a personal narrative for analysis, to arrive at implications that are not sufficiently grounded in the evidence.

Because darkness and dark clothing need not operate as symbols of death, and because the woman's expression is not unquestionably grief-stricken (she looks expressionless to us), a writer might well need more evidence to jump to a narrative about the feelings and situation of the mother (a kind of jump that personal/expressive writing can be quick to make because it typically seeks shared feeling and experience). If, for example, part of a coffin were showing from behind the curtain, or if there were an hourglass somewhere in the painting, a reader might more plausibly conclude that mourning and mortality are governing contexts.

A few rules are worth highlighting here:

1. The range of associations for explaining a given detail or word must be governed by context.

---

2. It's fine to use your personal reactions as a way to explore what a subject means, but take care not to make an interpretive leap stretch further than the actual details will support.

3. Because the tendency to transfer meanings from your own life onto a subject can lead you to ignore the details of the subject itself, you need always to be asking yourself, "What other explanations might plausibly account for this same pattern of detail?"

The Limits on Interpretation

Where do meanings come from? The first thing to understand about meanings is that they are *made*, not ready-made in the subject matter. They are the product of a transaction between a mind and the world, between a reader and a text or texts. That is, the making of meaning is a process to which the observer and the thing observed both contribute. It is not a product of either alone.

If meanings aren't ready-made, there to be found in the subject matter, what's to prevent people from making things mean whatever they want them to—say, for example, that *Whistler's Mother* is a painting about death, with the black-clad mother mourning the death of a loved one, perhaps a person who lived in the house represented in the painting on the wall? There are in fact limits on the meaning-making process.

- Meanings must be reasoned from sufficient evidence if they are to be judged plausible. Meanings can always be refuted by people who find fault with your reasoning or can cite conflicting evidence.
- Meanings, to have value outside one's own private realm of experience, have to make sense to other people. The assertion that Whistler's mother is an alien astronaut, for example, her long black dress concealing a third leg, is unlikely to be deemed acceptable by enough people to give it currency. This is to say that the relative value of interpretive meanings is socially (culturally) determined. Although people are free to say that things mean whatever they want them to mean, saying doesn't make it so.

Multiple Meanings and Interpretive Contexts

In the last section we demonstrated that there are certain limits on interpretation, chiefly that interpretation has to follow the rules of evidence. It is useful and reassuring to know that a person can't just make up meanings and say they are true simply because he or she says so. But it is also necessary to recognize that meanings are multiple. Very few things in life are so simple as to communicate only one thing.

Evidence usually will support more than one plausible interpretation. Consider, for example, a reading of *Whistler's Mother* that a person might produce if he or she began with noticing the actual title, *Arrangement in Grey and Black: The Artist's Mother*. From this starting point, a person might focus observation on the disposition of color exclusively and arrive at an interpretation that *Arrangement* is a painting about painting (which might then explain why there is also a painting on the wall). The figure of the mother then would have meaning only insofar as it contained the two colors mentioned in the painting's title, black and gray, and the painting's representational content (the aspects of life that it shows us) would be ignored. This is a promising and plausible idea for an interpretation. It makes use of different details from previous interpretations we've suggested, but it would also address some of the details already targeted (the dress, the curtain) from an entirely different context, focusing on the use and arrangement of color.

To generalize: two equally plausible interpretations can be made of the same thing. It is not the case that our first reading, focusing on the profile view of the mother and suggesting the painting's concern with mysterious separateness, is right, whereas the aesthetic view, building from the clue in the title, is wrong. They operate within different contexts. An interpretive context is a lens. Depending on the context you choose—preferably a context suggested by the evidence itself—you will see different things.

Regardless of how the context is arrived at, an important part of getting an interpretation accepted as plausible is to *argue for the appropriateness of the interpretive context you use*, not just the interpretation it takes you to.

Making a Thesis Evolve

WHAT A GOOD WORKING THESIS DOES

Promotes thinking: leads to greater precision about what things mean

Reduces scope: separates useful evidence from the welter of details

Provides direction: helps you decide what to talk about and what to talk about next

Contains tension: balances *this* against *that* in a form such as "although x, nevertheless y . . ."

WHAT A BAD THESIS DOES

Addicts you too early to a too-large idea, so that you stop actually seeing the evidence in its real-life complexity or thinking about the idea itself

Produces a demonstration rather than discovery of new ideas by making the same overly general point again and again about a range of evidence

Includes too much possible data without helping you see what's most important to talk about

What's Wrong with a Static Thesis

Basically, a static thesis is imprecise, overly general, and redundant. It asserts a meaning that is applied again and again as an answer, using different but similar pieces of evidence. Usually this answer is simple and single. It needs to be, because it is being asked to explain a lot, to contain so much evidence. The truth, though, is rarely either simple or single.

The static thesis—a broad label slapped on a bunch of examples—tends to produce *demonstrations*. Demonstrations point at something—"See?"—and then they're done with it. They're not interested in seeing *into* things, only looking at them from a distance to confirm a point so broad, such as "Exercise is good for you," that it was probably not worth offering as a thesis in the first place.

The staple of the demonstration form of paper writing is the five-paragraph form, which we critiqued earlier. The form predisposes the writer to begin with a BIG claim, such as "Environmentalism prevents economic growth," and then offer a paragraph on three examples (say, statutes that protect endangered wildlife, inhibit drilling for oil, and levy excessive fines on violators). Then the big claim simply gets repeated again, after a "Thus, we see . . .

At the least, such a thesis is inaccurate. It's too easy to find exceptions to the claim and also to question what its key words actually mean. Mightn't environmentalism also promote economic growth by, say, promoting tourism? And is the meaning of economic growth self-evident? Couldn't a short-term economic boon be a long-term disaster, as might be the case for oil exploration in the polar regions?

In sum, most of what typically goes wrong in using a thesis is the result of a writer leaping too quickly to a generalization that would do as a thesis, and then treating evidence *only* as something to be mustered in support of that idea. Simply repeating the same big idea keeps things too superficial. In papers that contain a static thesis, nothing happens to the claim itself: it doesn't grow, add to our knowledge, or generate new ideas.

A. Evolving a Thesis

THE RECIPROCAL RELATIONSHIP BETWEEN WORKING THESIS AND EVIDENCE: THE THESIS AS A CAMERA LENS

It's useful to think of the thesis as a camera lens that affects how we see the subject, what evidence we select, and what questions we ask about that evidence. But it's essential to understand that the subject being viewed also affects the lens. In good analytical writing, the analysis of evidence should also focus and refocus (bring about revision of) the thesis. Even in a final draft, writers are usually fine-tuning their governing idea in response to their analysis of evidence. The relationship between thesis and subject is thus *reciprocal* (see Figure 6.1).

In the terms of this analogy, very broad thesis statements, made up of imprecise (fuzzy) terms, make bad camera lenses. If your lens is insufficiently sharp, you are not likely to see much in your evidence. If you say, for example, that "the economic situation today is bad," you will at least have some sense of direction, but the imprecise terms *bad* and *economic situation* don't provide you with a focus clear enough to distinguish significant detail in your evidence. Without significant detail to analyze, you can't develop your thesis, either by showing readers what the thesis is good for (what it allows us to understand and explain) or by clarifying its terms.

Let's take one more brief example of a fuzzy-lens thesis and lay out a few basic moves for evolving it. Say that you're looking for a trend (or strand) in contemporary films you've seen and, as a working thesis, you claim that "Women in contemporary films are represented as being more sensitive than men." To avoid a mere demonstration and instead make this thesis evolve, you would need to

- query its key terms, asking yourself what these actually mean, and
- search for data that not only matched your claim but also didn't match it.

You'd more or less be assuming that you had overstated things, and you'd be looking for ways to press yourself to make further distinctions in your initial formulation, to make it less fuzzy.

Having claimed that the films show women as more sensitive than men, ask yourself what *sensitive* means, and by what criteria you are assessing its presence and absence. Is the overt expression of tender

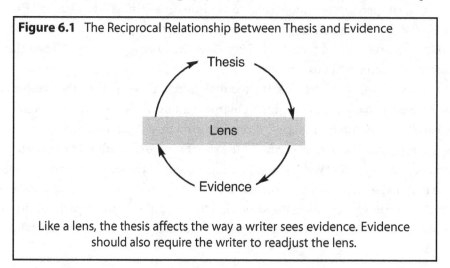

Figure 6.1 The Reciprocal Relationship Between Thesis and Evidence

Like a lens, the thesis affects the way a writer sees evidence. Evidence should also require the writer to readjust the lens.

feelings the only acceptable evidence for being sensitive? Couldn't men have less demonstrative ways of being sensitive? What is the best piece or two of evidence that men do show something like sensitivity in the films you're considering?

And surely you could also complicate that claim by locating it within a richer *context*. It's not enough to assert that women are represented as sensitive in the films. What are these films inviting us to think about their sensitivity? Are the women punished for it in the plots? Are they rewarded with being liked (approved of) by the films, even if this trait causes them problems?

Such considerations as these would require significant *reformulation* of the thesis. This procedure will normally be repeated several times, with each new discussion of significant evidence. For this reason you may find it useful to think of the claim-making aspect of a piece of writing not simply as a thesis, which implies that it is a settled thing, but rather as *a working thesis*, which suggests that the claim is in process, metamorphosing through a series of contexts within the paper.

By the end of the paper, the claim that "women are more sensitive than men" should have evolved into a more carefully defined and qualified statement that reflects the thinking you have done in your analysis of evidence. This is what good concluding paragraphs do; they reflect back on and reformulate your paper's initial position in light of the thinking you have done about it (see Figure 6.2).

You might ask, Isn't this reformulating of the thesis something a writer does *before* he or she writes the essay? Certainly some of it is accomplished in your exploratory drafting and note taking, and your revision process should weed out various false starts and dead ends. But your finished paper should include the evolutions of your thesis. To an extent, all good writing re-creates the chains of thought that lead writers to their conclusions. If you just listed your conclusions, your readers might rightly question how you arrived at them. The math routes of your movement from a tentative idea to a refined and substantiated theory should remain visible for readers to follow. (See "The Evolving Thesis in a Final Draft" later in this chapter for further discussion of how much thesis evolution to include in your final draft.)

A FIRST NOTE ON THE SHAPE OF THESIS STATEMENTS

Before we move on to concentrated applications of the procedure for making a thesis evolve, take a look back at the shape of the imprecise thesis statements used as examples in this chapter:

Environmentalism prevents economic growth.
The economic situation today is bad.
Women in contemporary films are represented as being more sensitive than men.

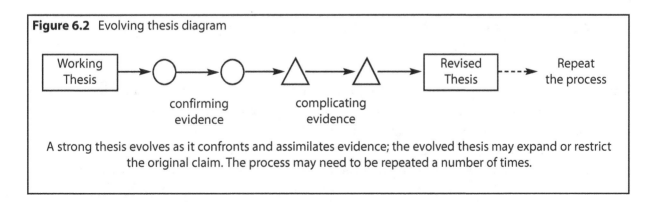

Figure 6.2 Evolving thesis diagram

A strong thesis evolves as it confronts and assimilates evidence; the evolved thesis may expand or restrict the original claim. The process may need to be repeated a number of times.

All three are simple, declarative sentences that offer very abstract assertions. That is, they are both grammatically and conceptually simple. More than that, they're *slack*—especially the first two, which stand alone, not in relation to anything else.

The very *shape* of these weak thesis statements is a warning sign. Most effective working theses, though they may begin more simply, achieve both grammatical and conceptual complexity as they evolve. Such theses contain tension, the balance of this against that; this degree, with that qualification. Often they begin with *although* or incorporate *however* or use an *appears to be about* x *but is actually about* y kind of formulation. Here, by contrast to the weak theses above, are three possible evolutions of the "sensitivity" thesis:

Although women cry more readily in contemporary films, the men, by not crying, seem to win the audience's favor.

The complications that fuel the plots in today's romantic comedies arise because women and men express their sensitivity so differently; the resolutions, however, rarely require the men to capitulate.

A spate of recent films has witnessed the emergence of the new "womanly" man as hero, and not surprisingly, his tender qualities seem to be the reason he attracts the female love interest.

Try this 6.1: Qualifying Overstated Claims

Using as a model of inquiry the treatment of the example thesis "Women in contemporary films are represented as being more sensitive than men," seek out complications in one of the overstated claims in the following list. These complications might inclde conflicting evidence (which you should specify) and questions about the meaning or appropriateness of key terms (again, which you should exemplify).

Illustrate a few of these complications, and then reformulate the claim in language that is more carefully qualified and accurate.

Welfare encourages recipients not to work.

Midwives are more caring than gynecologists.

Religious people are more moral than those who are not religious.

School gets in the way of education.

Herbal remedies are better than pharmaceutical ones.

The book is always better than the film.

Procedure for Making the Thesis Evolve through Successive Complications: The Example of *Educating Rita*

This section of the chapter presents an extended example that illustrates how the initial formulation of a thesis might evolve—through a series of complications—over the course of a draft. It closely follows in organization the "Six Steps for Making a Thesis Evolve."

Let's consider the stages you might go through within a more finished draft to evolve a thesis about a film. In *Educating Rita*, a working-class English hairdresser (Rita) wants to change her life by taking

SIX STEPS FOR MAKING A THESIS EVOLVE
1. Formulate an idea about your subject—a working thesis.
2. See how far you can make this thesis go in accounting for (confirming) evidence.
3. Locate complicating evidence that is not adequately accounted for by the thesis.
4. Make explicit the apparent mismatch between the thesis and selected evidence, asking and answering So what?
5. Reshape your claim to accommodate the evidence that hasn't fit.
6. Repeat steps 2, 3, 4, and 5 several times.

courses from a professor (Frank) at the local university, even though this move threatens her relationship with her husband (Denny), who burns her books and pressures her to quit school and get pregnant. Frank, she discovers, has his own problems: he's a divorced alcoholic who is bored with his life, bored with his privileged and complacent students, and bent on self-destruction. The film follows the growth of Frank and Rita's friendship and the changes it brings about in their lives. By the end of the film, each has left a limiting way of life behind and has set off in a seemingly more promising direction. She leaves her constricting marriage, passes her university examinations with honors, and begins to view her life in terms of choices; he stops drinking and sets off, determined but sad, to make a new start as a teacher in Australia.

Formulate an idea about your subject, a working thesis (step 1).

> **Working thesis:** *Educating Rita* celebrates the liberating potential of education.

The film's relatively happy ending and the presence of the word *educating* in the film's title make this thesis a reasonable opening claim.

See how far you can make this thesis go in accounting for evidence (step 2). The working thesis seems compatible, for example, with Rita's achievement of greater self-awareness and independence. You would go on to locate similar data that would support the idea that education is potentially liberating. She becomes more articulate, which allows her to free herself from otherwise disabling situations. She starts to think about other kinds of work she might do, rather than assuming that she must continue in the one job she has always done. She travels, first elsewhere in England and then to the Continent. So, the thesis checks out as viable: there is enough of a match with evidence to make it worth pursuing.

Locate evidence that is not adequately accounted for by the thesis and ask So what? about the apparent mismatch between the thesis and selected evidence (steps 3 and 4). Other evidence troubles the adequacy of the working thesis, however: Rita's education causes her to become alienated from her husband, her parents, and her social class; at the end of the film she is alone and unsure about her direction in life. In Frank's case, the thesis runs into even more problems. His boredom, drinking, and alienation seem to have been caused, at least in part, by his education rather than by his lack of it. He sees his book-lined study as a prison. Moreover, his profound knowledge of literature has not helped him control his life: he comes to class drunk, fails to notice or care that his girlfriend is having an affair with one of his colleagues, and asks his classes whether it is worth gaining all of literature if it means losing one's soul.

Reshape your claim to accommodate the evidence that hasn't fit (step 5). *Question: What are you to do?* You cannot convincingly argue that the film celebrates the liberating potential of education, because that thesis ignores such a significant amount of the evidence. Nor can you "switch sides" and argue that the film attacks education as life-denying and disabling, because this thesis is also only partially true.

What not to do. Faced with evidence that complicates your thesis, you should not assume that it is worthless and that you need to start over from scratch. View the "problem" you have discovered as an opportunity to modify your thesis rather than abandon it. After all, the thesis still fits a lot of significant evidence. Rita is arguably better off at the end of the film than at the beginning: we are not left to believe that she should have remained resistant to education, like her husband, Denny, whose world doesn't extend much beyond the corner pub.

What to do. Make apparent complications explicit—the film's seemingly contradictory attitudes about education—and then modify the wording of your thesis in a way that might resolve or explain these contradictions. You might, for example, be able to resolve an apparent contradiction between your initial thesis (the film celebrates the liberating potential of education) and the evidence by proposing that there is more than one version of education depicted in the film. You would, in short, start qualifying and clarifying the meaning of key terms in your thesis.

In this case, you could divide education as represented by the film into two kinds: enabling and stultifying. The next step in the development of your thesis would be to elaborate on how the film seeks to distinguish true and enabling forms of education from false and debilitating ones (as represented by the self-satisfied and status-conscious behavior of the supposedly educated people at Frank's university).

> **Revised thesis:** *Educating Rita* celebrates the liberating potential of enabling—in contrast to stultifying —education.

Repeat steps 2, 3, 4, and 5 (step 6). Having refined your thesis in this way, you would then repeat the step of seeing what the new wording allows you to account for in your evidence. The revised thesis might, for example, explain Frank's problems as being less a product of his education than of the cynical and pretentious versions of education that surround him in his university life. You could posit further that, with Rita as inspiration, Frank rediscovers at least some of his idealism about education.

What about Frank's emigration to Australia? If we can take Australia to stand for a newer world, one where education would be less likely to become the stale and exclusive property of a self-satisfied elite, then the refined version of the thesis would seem to be working well. In fact, given the possible thematic connection between Rita's working-class identity and Australia (associated, as a former frontier and English penal colony, with lower-class vitality as opposed to the complacency bred of class privilege), the thesis about the film's celebration of the contrast between enabling and stultifying forms of education could be sharpened further. You might propose, for example, that the film presents institutional education as desperately in need of frequent doses of "real life" (as represented by Rita and Australia)—infusions of working-class pragmatism, energy, and optimism—if it is to remain healthy and open, as opposed to becoming the oppressive property of a privileged social class. This is to say that the film arguably exploits stereotypical assumptions about social class.

> **Revised thesis:** *Educating Rita* celebrates the liberating potential of enabling education, defined as that which remains open to healthy doses of working-class, real-world infusions.

Similarly, you can make your supporting ideas (those on which your thesis depends) more accurate and less susceptible to oversimplification by seeking evidence that might challenge their key terms. Sharpening the language of your supporting assertions will help you develop your thesis.

Consider, for example, the wording of the supporting idea that *Educating Rita* has a happy ending. Some qualification of this idea through consideration of possibly conflicting evidence could produce an adjustment in the first part of the working thesis, that the film celebrates education and presents it as liberating. At the end of the film, Frank and Rita walk off in opposite directions down long, empty airport corridors. Though promising to remain friends, the two do not become a couple. This closing emphasis on Frank's and Rita's alienation from their respective cultures, and the film's apparent insistence on the necessity of each going on alone, significantly qualifies the happiness of the "happy ending."

Once you have complicated your interpretation of the ending, you will again need to modify your thesis in accord with your new observations. Does the film simply celebrate education if it also presents it as being, to some degree, incompatible with conventional forms of happiness? By emphasizing the necessity of having Frank and Rita each go on alone, the film may be suggesting that to be truly liberating, education—as opposed to its less honest and more comfortable substitutes—inevitably produces and even requires a certain amount of loneliness and alienation. Shown in Figure 6.3 are the successive revisions of the thesis.

> **Final version of thesis:** *Educating Rita* celebrates the liberating potential of enabling education (kept open to real-world, working-class energy) but also acknowledges its potential costs in loneliness and alienation.

Try this 6.2: Tracking a Thesis

As should be clear now, various versions of the thesis recur throughout a piece of writing, usually with increasing specificity, complication, and grammatical complexity. The four thesis statements on *Educating Rita* illustrate this pattern of recurrence clearly. One of the best ways to teach yourself how and where to locate statements of the thesis in your own writing is to track the thesis in a piece of reading. Ideally you should choose an essay or article used in one of your courses, because this exercise will also powerfully increase your understanding of the reading. Use a highlighter to mark the evolutions. Where in the essay do you find the thesis? How has it changed in each recurrence? In response to what complication?

B. Using the Evolving Thesis to Organize the Final Draft

Having achieved a final version of a thesis, *what next?* Why wouldn't a writer just offer the last and fullest statement of the thesis in his or her first paragraph and then prove it?

Usually it's neither possible nor desirable to encapsulate in the opening sentences what it will actually take the whole paper to explain. The position articulated in the fully evolved thesis is typically too complex to be stated intelligibly and concisely in the introduction. But more, if you think of an essay as an act of thinking, then the evolutions of the thesis record the history of your various changes in thinking as you confronted evidence. If your readers get to see these, they are far more likely to go along with you, literally to follow your trains of thought.

Before treating these matters in more detail, however, let us nail down a general answer to the question of thesis locations.

- The first articulation of the working thesis almost always occurs late in the opening paragraph or early in the second paragraph of a piece, after the writer has presented the problem or question that establishes the tension the thesis aims to resolve, and given some kind of context for it.

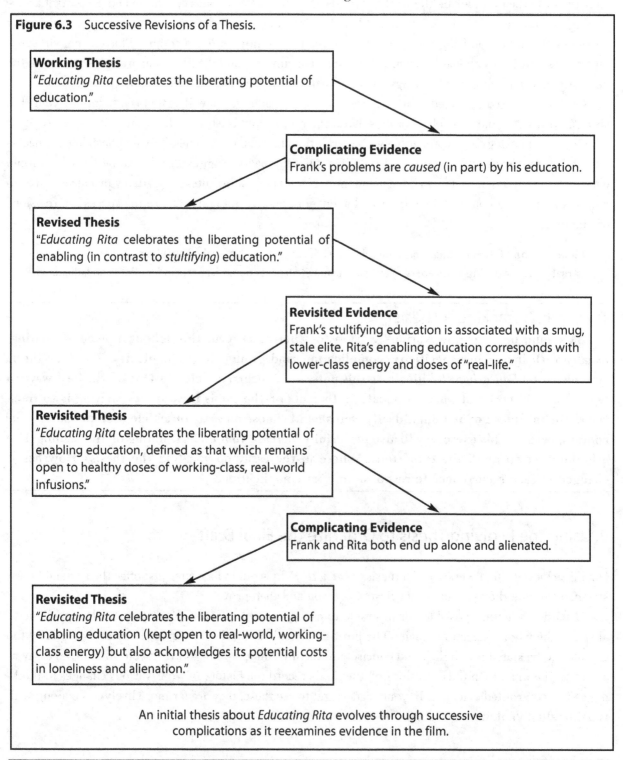

Figure 6.3 Successive Revisions of a Thesis.

Working Thesis
"*Educating Rita* celebrates the liberating potential of education."

Complicating Evidence
Frank's problems are *caused* (in part) by his education.

Revised Thesis
"*Educating Rita* celebrates the liberating potential of enabling (in contrast to *stultifying*) education."

Revisited Evidence
Frank's stultifying education is associated with a smug, stale elite. Rita's enabling education corresponds with lower-class energy and doses of "real-life."

Revisited Thesis
"*Educating Rita* celebrates the liberating potential of enabling education, defined as that which remains open to healthy doses of working-class, real-world infusions."

Complicating Evidence
Frank and Rita both end up alone and alienated.

Revisited Thesis
"*Educating Rita* celebrates the liberating potential of enabling education (kept open to real-world, working-class energy) but also acknowledges its potential costs in loneliness and alienation."

An initial thesis about *Educating Rita* evolves through successive complications as it reexamines evidence in the film.

- Subsequent articulations of the thesis usually occur at points of transition, typically at paragraph openings following the analysis of complicating evidence. These thesis evolutions are often overtly marked as such—the writer tells readers that on the basis of this analysis, it is necessary to amend the governing claim. This kind of explicit updating has the added benefit of providing unity to the essay, using the thesis as a kind of spine.
- The final statement of the thesis occurs in the concluding paragraph, or perhaps the penultimate one. It is usually offered in clear relationship to the terms offered in the introduction, so the reader is offered a last vision of where the essay has traveled.

A more complete answer to the questions of where and how to locate versions of the thesis in a final draft involves two related issues: (1) the location of the thesis statement in relation to the conventional shapes of argument—induction and deduction—and (2) the customary location of the thesis according to the protocols (ways of proceeding) of different disciplines. We will treat each of these in its turn.

The Evolving Thesis and Common Thought Patterns: Deduction and Induction

Put simply, in a deductive paper a fairly full-fledged version of the thesis appears at the beginning; in an inductive paper, it appears at the end (see Figure 6.4, A and B).

As a thought process, deduction reasons from a general principle (assumed to be true) to the particular case. It introduces this principle up front and then uses it to select and interpret evidence. For example, a deductive paper might state in its first paragraph that attitudes toward and rules governing sexuality in a given culture can be seen, at least in part, to have economic causes. The paper might then apply this principle, already assumed to be true, to the codes governing sexual behavior in several cultures or several kinds of sexual behavior in a single culture.

A good deductive argument is, however, more than a mechanical application or matching exercise of general claim and specific details that are explained by it. Deductive reasoning uses the evidence to draw out the implications—what logicians term *inferring the consequences*—of the claim. The general principle explains selected features of particular cases, and *reciprocally*, the evidence brings out implications in the principle.

Thus, the general principle stated at the beginning of the paper and the idea stated as the paper's conclusion are not the same. Rather, the conclusion presents the (evolved) idea that the writer has arrived at through the application of the principle.

An inductively organized paper typically begins not with a principle already accepted as true but with particular data for which it seeks to generate some explanatory principle.

Whereas deduction moves by applying a generalization to particular cases, induction moves from the observation of individual cases to the formation of a general principle. Because all possible cases can obviously never be examined—every left-handed person, for example, if one wishes to theorize that left-handed people are better at spatial thinking than right-handers—the principle (or thesis) arrived at through inductive reasoning always remains open to doubt.

Nevertheless, the thesis of an inductive paper is generally deemed acceptable if a writer can demonstrate that the theory is based on a reasonably sized sampling of representative instances. (This matter of representativeness was taken up in our earlier discussion of 10 on 1.) Suffice it to say that a child who arrives at the thesis that all orange food tastes bad on the basis of squash and carrots has not based that theory on an adequate sampling of available evidence.

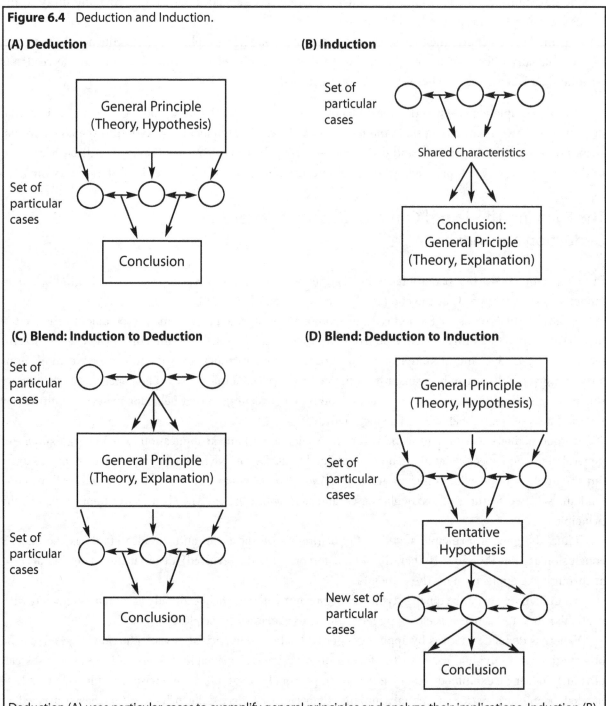

Figure 6.4 Deduction and Induction.

Deduction (A) uses particular cases to exemplify general principles and analyze their implications. Induction (B) constructs general principles from the analysis of particular cases. In practice, analytical thinking and writing blend deduction and induction and start either with particular cases (C) or general principle (D).

What we hope this discussion makes clear is that whether your analysis is primarily inductive or deductive, the thesis will undergo evolution as it confronts evidence. What still needs to be understood, though, is that in most cases induction and deduction operate in tandem (see Figure 6.4, C and D). It's true that in some disciplines (philosophy, for example) the deductive pattern of argument prevails, but not exclusively: the analysis of evidence, though clearly designed to reflect a general principle, will also lead to new formulations that will modify the general principle in various ways.

It is in the nature of analysis to move between the particular and the general, regardless of which comes first. Whether the overall shape of the analysis—its mode of progression—is primarily inductive or deductive, it will still *gain in complexity* from beginning to end. The statement with which you begin is not also the end (see Figure 6.4).

Try this 6.3: Formulating an Inductive Principle

Study a group of like things inductively. You might, for example, use greeting cards aimed at women versus greeting cards aimed at men, a group of poems by one author, or ads for one kind of product (jeans) or aimed at one target group (teenage girls).

Make use of the looking-for-patterns heuristic (see the Method in Chapter 2) to compile and organize a set of significant details about the data, and then leap to a general claim about the group that you think is interesting and reasonably accurate. This generalization is your inductive principle. Then use the principle to examine deductively more data of the same kind, exploring its implications as you evolve it more accurately.

THE EVOLVING THESIS AS HYPOTHESIS AND CONCLUSION IN THE NATURAL AND SOCIAL SCIENCES

A thesis functions differently depending on the academic discipline—whether it must be stated in full at the outset, for example, and what happens to it between the beginning of the paper and the end. The differences appear largest as you move back and forth between courses in the humanities and courses in the natural and certain of the social sciences.

Broadly speaking, papers in the humanities are inclined to begin inductively, and papers in the natural and social sciences deductively. The natural and social sciences generally use a pair of terms, *hypothesis* and *conclusion*, for the single term thesis. Because writing in the sciences is patterned according to the scientific method, writers in disciplines such as biology and psychology must report how the original thesis (hypothesis) was tested against empirical evidence and then conclude on this basis whether or not the hypothesis was confirmed.

The gap between this way of thinking about the thesis and the concept of an evolving thesis is not as large as it may seem. The scientific method is in sync with one of the chapter's main points, that something must happen to the thesis between the introduction and the conclusion, so that the conclusion does more than just reassert what was already asserted in the beginning.

Analogously, in a scientific paper, the hypothesis is tested against evidence, the results of which allow the writer to draw conclusions about the hypothesis's validity. Although the hypothesis does not change (or evolve), the testing of it and subsequent interpretation of those results produce commentary on and, often, qualifications of the paper's central claim.

In the natural and social sciences, successive reformulations of the thesis are less likely to be recorded and may not even be expressly articulated. But, as in all disciplines, the primary analytical activity in the sciences is to repeatedly reconsider the assumptions upon which a conclusion is based.

THE EVOLVING THESIS AND INTRODUCTORY AND CONCLUDING PARAGRAPHS

If you are not using the hypothesis/conclusion format, your final drafts could often begin by predicting the evolution of their theses. Thus, the *Educating Rita* paper might open by using a version of the seems-to-be-about-*x* gambit, claiming that at first glance the film seems to celebrate the liberating potential of education. You could then lay out the evidence for this view and proceed to complicate it in the ways we've discussed.

What typically happens is that you lead (usually at the end of the first paragraph or at the beginning of the second) with the best version of your thesis that you can come up with that will be understandable to your readers without a lengthy preamble. If you find yourself writing a page-long introductory paragraph to get to your initial statement of thesis, try settling for a simpler articulation of your central idea in its first appearance. As you move through the paper, substantiate, elaborate on, test, and qualify your paper's opening gambit.

The most important thing to do in the introductory paragraph of an analytical paper is to lay out a genuine issue, which is to say, something that seems to be at stake in whatever you are studying. Ideally, you should select a complex issue—one not easily resolved, seeming to have some truth on both sides—and not an overly general one. Otherwise you run the risk of writing a paper that proves the obvious or radically oversimplifies.

Set up this issue as quickly and concretely as you can, avoiding generic (fits anything) comments, throat clearing, and review-style evaluations. As a general rule, you should assume that readers of your essay will need to know on page 1—preferably by the end of your first paragraph—what your paper is attempting to resolve or negotiate.

The first paragraph does not need to—and usually can't—offer your conclusion; it will take the body of your paper to accomplish that. It should, however, provide a quick look at particular details that set up the issue. Use these details to generate a theory, a *working hypothesis*, about whatever it is you think is at stake in the material. The rest of the paper will test and develop this theory.

Your concluding paragraph will offer the more carefully qualified and evolved version of your thesis that the body of your paper has allowed you to arrive at. Rather than just summarize and restate what you said in your introduction, the concluding paragraph should leave readers with what you take to be your single best insight, and it should put what you have had to say into some kind of perspective. See Chapter 8 for a more extended discussion of introductions and conclusions.

VOICES FROM ACROSS THE CURRICULUM

Recognizing Your Thesis

For an analytical interpretive historical essay, *thesis* is a conventional term and one of much value. The thesis usually is that point of departure from the surfaces of evidence to the underlying significance, or problems, a given set of sources reveal to the reader and writer. In most cases, the thesis is best positioned up front, so that the writer's audience has a sense of what lies ahead and why it is worth reading on. I say *usually* and *in most cases* because the hard and fast rule should not take precedence over the inspirational manner in which a thesis can be presented. But the inspiration is not to be sought after at the price of the thesis itself. It is my experience, in fact, that if inspiration strikes, one realizes it only after the fact.

Recognizing a thesis can be extremely difficult. It can often be a lot easier to talk "about" what one is writing than to say succinctly what the thrust of one's discussion is. I sometimes ask students to draw a line at the end of a paper after they have finished it, and then write one, at most two sentences, saying what they most want to tell their readers. My comment on that postscript frequently is "Great statement of your thesis. Just move it up to your first paragraph."

—Ellen Poteet, Professor of History

The Function of Conclusions

Like the introduction, the conclusion has a key social function: it escorts the readers out of the paper, just as the introduction has escorted them in. What do readers want as they leave the textual world you have taken them through? Although the form and length of the conclusion depend on the purpose and disciplinary conventions of the particular paper, it is possible to generalize a set of shared expectations for the conclusion across the curriculum. In some combination most readers want three things: a judgment, a culmination, and a send-off.

> **Judgment**—The conclusion is the site for final judgment on whatever question or issue or problem the paper has focused upon. In most cases, this judgment occurs in overt connection with the introduction, often repeating some of its key terms. The conclusion normally reconsiders the question raised by the opening hypothesis and, however tentatively, rules yea or nay. It also explicitly revisits the introductory claim for why the topic matters.

> **Culmination**—More than simply summarizing what has preceded or reasserting your main point, the conclusion needs to culminate. The word "culminate" is derived from the Latin *columen*, meaning "top or summit." To culminate is to reach the highest point, and it implies a mountain (in this case, of information and analysis) that you have scaled. When you culminate a paper in a conclusion, you bring things together and ascend to one final statement of your thinking.

> **Send-Off**—The climactic effects of judgment and culmination provide the basis for the send-off. The send-off is both social and conceptual, a final opening outward of the topic that leads the reader out of the paper with something further to think about. As is suggested by most of the professors in the accompanying "Voices from Across the Curriculum" boxes, the conclusion needs to move beyond the close analysis of data that has occupied the body of the paper into a kind of speculation that the writer has earned the right to formulate.

Here is an example of a conclusion that contains a final judgment, a culmination, and a send-off. The paper, a student's account of what she learned about science from doing research in biology, opens by claiming that, to the apprentice, "science assumes an impressive air of complete reliability, especially to its distant human acquaintances." Having been attracted to science by the popular view that it proceeds infallibly, she arrives at quite a different final assessment:

> All I truly know from my research is that the infinite number of factors that can cause an experiment to go wrong make tinkering a lab skill just as necessary as reading a buret. A scientist can eventually figure out a way to collect the data she wants if she has the patience to repeatedly recombine her materials and tools in slightly different ways. A researcher's success, then, often depends largely on her being lucky enough to locate, among all the possibilities, the one procedure that works.

> Aided more by persistence and fortune than by formal training, I evolved a method that produced credible results. But, like the tests from which it derived, the success of that method is probably also highly specific to a certain experimental environment and so is valid only for research involving borosilicate melts treated with hydrofluoric and boric acids. I've discovered a principle, but it's hardly a universal one: reality is too

complex to allow much scientific generalization. Science may appear to sit firmly on all-encompassing truths, but the bulk of its weight actually rests on countless little rules tailored for particular situations.

This writer deftly interweaves the original claim from her introduction—that "science assumes an impressive air of complete reliability"—into a final *judgment* of her topic, delivered in the last sentence. This judgment is also a *culmination*, as it moves from her account of doing borosilicate melts to the small but acute generalization that "little rules tailored for particular situations" rather than "all-encompassing truths" provide the mainstay of scientific research. Notice that *a culmination does not need to make a grand claim in order to be effective.* In fact, the relative smallness of the final claim, especially in contrast to the sweeping introductory position about scientific infallibility, ultimately provides a *send-off* made effective by its unexpected understatement.

WAYS OF CONCLUDING

The three professors quoted on pages 230–232 all advise some version of the judgment/culmination/send-off combination. The first professor stresses the send-off.

Although it is true that the conclusion is the place for "broader ramifications," this phrase should not be understood as a call for a global generalization. As the professor in the "Voices from Across the Curriculum" box suggests, often the culmination represents a final limiting of a paper's original claim.

THREE STRATEGIES FOR WRITING EFFECTIVE CONCLUSIONS

There is striking overlap in the advice offered in the cross-disciplinary "voices." All caution that the conclusion should provide more than a restatement of what you've already said. All suggest that the conclusion should, in effect, serve as the introduction to some "larger 'mental' paper out there" (as one professor

VOICES FROM ACROSS THE CURRICULUM

Expanding Possibilities in the Conclusion

I tell my students that too many papers "just end," as if the last page or so were missing. I tell them the importance of ending a work. One could summarize main points, but I tell them this is not heavy lifting. They could raise issues not addressed (but hinted at) in the main body: "given this, one could consider that." I tell them that a good place for reflection might be a concluding section in which they take the ball and run: react, critique, agree, disagree, recommend, suggest, or predict.

I help them by asking, "where does the paper seem to go *after* it ends on paper?" That is, I want the paper to live on even though the five pages are filled. I don't want to suddenly stop thinking or reacting just because I've read the last word on the bottom of page 5. I want to experience, as if the paper is still with me.

I believe the ending should be an expansion on or explosion of possibilities, sort of like an introduction to some much larger "mental" paper out there. I sometimes encourage students to see the concluding section as an option to introduce ideas that can't be dealt with now. Sort of a "Having done this, I would want to explore boom, boom, boom if I were to continue further." Here the students can critique and recommend ("Having seen 'this,' one wonders 'that'").

—Frederick Norling, Professor of Business

There must be a summation. What part did the stock market crash of 1929 play in the onset of the Great Depression? Lets hear that conclusion one more time. Again, but now in an abbreviated form, what's the evidence? What are the main ambiguities that remain? Has your paper raised any new questions for future research? Are there any other broader ramifications following in the wake of your paper?

—James Marshall, Professor of Economics

puts it) beyond the confines of your own paper. By consensus, the professors make three recommendations for conclusions:

1. *Pursue implications.* Reason inductively from your particular study to consider broader issues, such as the study's practical consequences or applications, or future-oriented issues, such as avenues for further research. To unfold implications in this way is to broaden the view from the here and now of your paper by looking outward to the wider world and forward to the future.

2. *Come full circle.* Unify your paper by interpreting the results of your analysis in light of the context you established in your introduction.

3. *Identify limitations.* Acknowledge restrictions of method or focus in your analysis, and qualify your conclusion (and its implications) accordingly.

Solving Typical Problems in Conclusions

The primary challenge in writing conclusions, it should now be evident, lies in finding a way to culminate your analysis without claiming either too little or too much. There are a number of fairly common problems to guard against if you are to avoid either of these two extremes.

REDUNDANCY

In Chapter 5 we lampooned an exaggerated example of the five-paragraph form for constructing its conclusion by stating "Thus, we see" and then repeating the introduction verbatim. The result is *redundancy*. As you've seen, it's a good idea to refer back to the opening, but it's a bad idea just to reinsert it mechanically. Instead, reevaluate what you said there in light of where you've ended up, repeating only key words or phrases from the introduction. This kind of *selective repetition* is a desirable way of achieving unity and will keep you from making one of two opposite mistakes—either repeating too much or bringing up a totally new point in the conclusion.

RAISING A TOTALLY NEW POINT

Raising a totally new point can distract or bewilder a reader. This problem often arises out of a writer's praiseworthy desire to avoid repetition. As a rule, you can guard against the problem by making sure that you have clearly expressed the conceptual link between your central conclusion and any implications you may draw. *An implication is not a totally new point but rather one that follows from the position you have been analyzing.*

Similarly, although a capping judgment or send-off may appear for the first time in your concluding paragraph, it should have been *anticipated* by the body of your paper. Conclusions often indicate where you think you (or an interested reader) may need to go next, but you don't actually go there. In a paper on the economist Milton Friedman, for example, if you think that another economist offers a useful way of critiquing him, you probably should not introduce this person for the first time in your conclusion.

OVERSTATEMENT

Many writers are confused over how much they should claim in the conclusion. Out of the understandable (but mistaken) desire for a grand (rather than a modest and qualified) culmination, writers sometimes *overstate* the case. That is, they assert more than their evidence has proven or even suggested. Must a conclusion arrive at some comprehensive and final answer to the question that your paper has analyzed? Depending on the question and the disciplinary conventions, you may need to come down exclusively on one side or another. In a great many cases, however, the answers with which you conclude can be more moderate. Especially in the humanities, good analytical writing seeks to unfold successive layers of implication, so it's not even reasonable for you to expect neat closure. In such cases, you are usually better off qualifying your final judgments, drawing the line at points of relative stability.

What to Do with the Reading: Avoiding the Matching Exercise

What does it mean "to do something with the reading"? Obviously, you can paraphrase, summarize, or do a focused freewrite with it, but these exercises aim primarily to establish a more accurate, active, and rich understanding of what the reading is doing and saying. That's why they are included under the heading "How to Read: Words Matter." When, by contrast, you *do* something with the reading, you use it for purposes that are different from the aims of the reading itself. This distinction holds for all kinds of reading, not just the academic or literary varieties. In a guide to bike repair, you might paraphrase the directions for replacing the brakes to make sure your understanding of this complex process is sufficiently clear. But if you use the knowledge you've gained to fix the brakes on some other machine, adapting what you've learned, you'll be doing something with the reading.

Much of the rest of this book suggests ways of negotiating what you read. In Chapter 12, for example, we concentrate on how to use secondary research. For now, we will discuss four basic approaches to doing things with the reading:

- applying a reading as a lens for examining something else
- comparing one reading with another
- using a reading as a model for writing
- uncovering the assumptions in a reading—where the piece is "coming from"

Applying a Reading as a Lens

Problem: A matching exercise, a mere demonstration of applicability.
Solution: Emphasize the shift in context, and then seek out areas of dissonance to analyze.

We apply what we read all the time. It's a standard academic assignment. You read an article on gender and blue jeans and then connect its ideas to something else—how, for example, magazine ads represent jeans-wearing with respect to gender. Or you study Freud's *The Interpretation of Dreams* and then analyze a dream of your own or a friend's as you project what Freud would have done. Or you apply his theory of repression in the behavior of a character in a novel or to some newfound realization about your mother's occasional bouts of frenzied housecleaning or your father's zealous weeding when he's upset. Freud thus becomes a *lens* for seeing the subject.

But what about taking an article on liberation theology as practiced by certain Catholic priests in Latin America and applying it to the rise of Islamic fundamentalism in the Middle East? Or for that matter, the directions for fixing the brakes on a bicycle to the analogous task on a car? Obviously, the original texts may be somewhat useful, but there are also significant differences between the two religious movements and between the two kinds of brakes.

So what should you do? When using a reading as a lens for better seeing what is going on in something you are studying, assume that the match between the lens and your subject will never be exact. It is often in the area where things don't match up exactly that you will find your best opportunity for having ideas.

Think about how lens A both fits and does not fit subject B: use the differences to develop your analysis.

The big problem with way most people apply a reading is that they do so too indiscriminately, too generally. They essentially construct *a matching exercise* in which each of a set of ideas drawn from text A is made to equate with a corresponding element (an idea or a fact) from subject B, often in virtual list-like fashion. Matching exercises are more useful in some contexts than in in others (great for fixing your bike's brakes, less so for analyzing your parents). At their worst, matching exercises are static, mechanical, and inaccurate. This is because they concentrate on similarities and forget the rest. As a result, the lens screens out what it cannot bring into focus, and the writer applying it distorts what he or she sees. Like an optometrist figuring out the new prescription for your glasses, you need to constantly adjust the lens whenever you bring it to new material. Don't just slap on A: really think about how it both fits *and* doesn't fit B.

Remember that whenever you apply lens A to a new subject B, you are taking A from its original context and using its ideas in at least somewhat different circumstances for at least somewhat different purposes. How does this shift change things, and thus, how may it require you to refocus the lens? Freud's theory of repression wasn't actually talking about your father, after all. The goal is not to dismiss Freud but to adjust his thinking to the particular case. There's always the danger that the reading you're appying will become a club to bludgeon your subject into submission.

Applying a Reading as a Lens: An Example Here is an excerpted version of a student paper that uses the theoretical lens of racial difference to examine Shakespeare's *The Tempest*. The writer considers the way the fatherly power figure and sorcerer Prospero, the ruler of the island where he has been shipwrecked, treats the creature Caliban, whom he finds there and enslaves. We have put inside brackets some commentary on how the writer applies the lens. Brackers and elllipses [. . .] indicate where we have abridged the essay.

> In their *Introduction to Literature, Criticism, and Theory*, Andrew Bennett and Nicholas Royle devote one chapter to the theme of "Racial Difference." They begin this chapter with a reference to Charlotte Bronte's novel *Jane Eyre*, and from this standpoint, they discuss a character in the book named Bertha, a West Indian Creole bound by chains in her white husband's attic. Of a scene in the narrative—told by the white female narrator—wherein Bertha's appearance is described, they write: "No longer a woman, Bertha is the other of humanity, unrecognizable as human, a beast with a purely animal physiognomy. Almost invisible, Bertha cannot be seen. Invisibility, as this suggests [. . .] is the condition of racial otherness" (199). [The writer begins by introducing the theoretical lens.]

> It is in such a way that Prospero's narrative portrays Caliber. As *The Tempest* was initially performed in seventeenth-century England, the audience to whom Prospero delivers his epilogue is primarily, if not fully, white—thus, racially homogeneous. And as Bennett and Royle further remind us, "Western humanism necessarily defines itself through racial otherness, by constructing a racial other which then stands in opposition to the humanity of the racially homogeneous" (201). Taking this into account, we begin to see how the construction of Caliban as his nonhuman other, by blatant contrast, could make Prospero seem all the more human to his racially alike audience. [Here the writer applies the theory. Note how he takes care to differentiate the context, suggesting a particularly seventeenth-century reading of the racism.]

The narrative achieves this end by utilizing the speech of several characters in the play to represent Caliban's behavior, nature, and physiognomy as decisively nonhuman. This narratological effect is carried out in several ways, mostly through appeals to a colonialist audience: by the portrayal of Caliban as verbally belligerent; by asserting that he once tried to rape Prospero's virgin daughter Miranda; by having nearly every character he encounters regard him as a monster on account of his appearance; and by scripting nearly every character, including Caliban himself, to believe that his nature is naturally that of a slave for the colonialist project. [The writer now moves confidently beyond the theoretical reading into his own analysis of Shakespeare's text.]

[. . .] Thus, Calibans physiognomy in this colony is that of a monster. Such a reference is made numerous times throughout the narrative. In the second scene of the second act, we find several malicious racial slurs referring to Caliban, which in Prospero's narrative are delivered humorously by the drunken butler and jester, Stephano and Trinculo respectively. When Trinculo encounters Caliban lying motionless upon the ground he observes: "What have we here, a man or a fish? Dead or alive? A fish, he smells like a fish, a very ancient and fishlike smell" (II, ii, 24–26). Soon thereafter, both Trinculo and Stephano refer to Caliban as a "mooncalf" (II, ii, 101, 106); by this they are referring to him as monstrous or as a freak. [As the essay nears its end, the writer has begun to focus on the details for making his case about the play's incorporation of Elizabethan racism.]

This is an effective application of a theoretical lens to open up a text to analysis from a particular interpretive context. The next step the writer might take if he were to extend the discussion would be to ponder the ways that subject B does *not* fit lens A. So what, for example, that Caliban is not "invisible" (199)? And does the play in any way contradict the quote from page 201 by, say, humanizing Caliban despite Prospero's attempts to dehumanize him? Nonetheless, the writer has done very well to recognize and then develop the implictions of the different historical context.

Try this 4.6: Using a Quotation as a Lens

Using the preceding paper excerpt as a model, apply the following generalization about talk shows to a talk show of your choice: "These shows obviously offer a distorted vision of America, thrive on feeling rather than thought, and worship the sound-byte rather than the art of conversation" (Stark 243). Alternatively, take any general claim you find in your reading and apply it to some other text or subject. Either way, strive to produce several paragraphs in which you avoid the matching exercise and instead probe both lens A and subject B.

Comparing and Contrasting One Reading with Another

Problem: Stopping too soon, with only a list of similarities and differences.
Solution: Look for difference within similarity or for similarity despite difference.

Comparing and contrasting is another traditional assignment done with readings, that falls flat when it turns into a mechanical matching exercise. Comparing readings resembles applying a reading as a lens. These activities are not intended as ends in themselves; they almost always contribute to some larger process of understanding.

The rationale for working comparatively is that you can usually discover ideas about a reading much more easily when you are not viewing it in isolation. You can observe it from a different perspective, in relation to something else. When used in this way, the comparison is usually not a 50-50 split; you've moved to a comparison of A with B because you want to better understand A.

In short, a good comparison should open up a reading, not close it down. It does more than demonstrate that you've "done the reading." We're all completely familiar with the formulaic conclusions to the comparisons produced by the matching-exercise mentality: "Thus we see there are many similarities and differences between A and B." Perfunctory, pointless, and inert lists: that's what you get if you stop the process of comparing and contrasting too soon, before you've focused and explored somethign interesting that you notice.

How do you avoid the ubiquitous matching-exercise habit? Here are three guidelines for productively comparing A with B:

1. Focus the comparison to give it a point. A comparison won't have a point inherently—you need to consciously give it one. It's often useful to assume that what you have originally taken for a point has not yet gone far enough and is still too close to summary. Rather than sticking with a range of broad comparisons, try to focus on a key comparison, one that you find interesting or revealing. (Looking for patterns, Notice and focus, and other tools can help you select your focus.) Although narrowing the focus in this way might seem to eliminate other important areas of consideration, in fact it usually allows you to incorporate at least some of these other areas in a more tightly connected, less list-like fashion.

If, to return to an earlier example, you were to compare the representations of the Boston Tea Party in British and American history texts, you would *begin but not stop* with identifying similarities and differences. The goal of your reading would be to focus on some particular matches that seem especially revealing—for example, that British and American texts trace the economic background of the incident in different ways. Then, in response to the So what? question, you could attempt to develop some expanation of what these differences reveal and why they are significant. You might, for example, decide that the British texts view the matter from a more global economic perspective, whereas American texts emphasize nationalism.

2. Look for significant difference between A and B, given their similarity. One of the best ways to arrive at a meaningful and interesting focus is to follow a principle that we call *looking for difference within similarity*. The procedure is simple but virtually guaranteed to produce a focused idea.

a. First, deal with the similarity. Identify what you take to be the essential similarity and then ask and answer, So what? Why is this similarity significant?

b. Then, in this context, identify the differences that you notice.

c. Choose one difference you find particularly revealing or interesting, and again ask, So what? What is the significance of this difference?

You can repeat this procedure with a range of key similarities and differences. Can you think of ways that the various differences are connected?

The phrase *difference within similarity* is to remind you that once you have started your thinking by locating apparent similarities, you can usually refine that thinking by pursuing significant, though often less obvious, distinctions among the similar things. In Irish studies, for example, scholars characteristically acknowledge the extent to which contemporary Irish culture is the product of colonization. To this extent, Irish culture shares certain traits with other former colonies in Africa, Asia, Latin America, and elsewhere.

But instad of simply demonstrating how Irish culture fits the general pattern of colonialism, these scholars also isolate the ways that Ireland *does not fit* the model. They focus, for example, on how its close geographical proximity and racial similarity to England, its colonizer, have distinguished the kinds of problems it encounters today from those characteristic of the more generalized model of colonialism. In effect, looking for difference within similarity has led them to locate and analyze the anomalies. (See the end of the next chapter for an extended example of looking for difference within similarity.)

3. Look for unexpected similarity hetween A and B, given their difference. A corollary of the preceeding principle is that you should focus on *unexpected similarity rather than obvious difference.* The fact that in the Bush presidency Republicans differ from Democrats on environmental policy is probably a less promising focal point than their surprising agreement on violating the so-called lockbox policy against tapping Social Security funds to finance government programs. Most readers would expect the political parties to differ on the environment, and a comparison of their positions could lead you to do little more than summarizing. But a surprising similarity, like an unexpected difference, necessarily raises questions for you to pursue: do the parties' shared positions against the lockbox policy, for example, share the same motives?

What to Do with Secondary Sources

First, by way of definition, we use the terms *source* and *secondary source* interchangeably to designate ideas and information about your subject that you find in the work of other writers. Secondary sources allow you to gain a richer, more informed, and complex vantage point on your *primary sources*. Here's how primary and secondary sources can be distinguished: if you were writing a paper on the philosopher Nietzsche, his writing would be your primary source, and critical commentaries on his work would be your secondary sources. If, however, you were writing on the poet Yeats, who read and was influenced by Nietzsche, a work of Nietzsche's philosophy would become a secondary source of yours on your primary source, Yeats's poetry.

"Source Anxiety" and What to Do About It

Typically, inexperienced writers either use sources as "answers"—they let the sources do too much of their thinking—or ignore them altogether as a way of avoiding "losing their own ideas." Both of these approaches are understandable but inadequate. We will take up the first of these in some detail in a moment, but for now let's concentrate on the second, ignoring sources altogether.

Confronted with the seasoned views of experts in a discipline, you may well feel that there is nothing left for you to say because it has all been said before or, at least, it has been said by people who greatly outweigh you in reputation and experience. This anxiety explains why so many writers surrender to the role of conduit for the voices of the experts, providing conjunctions between quotations. So why not avoid what other people have said? Won't this avoidance ensure that your ideas will be original and that, at the same time, you will be free from the danger of getting brainwashed by some "expert"?

The answer is "no." If you don't consult what others have said, you run at least two risks: you will waste your time reinventing the wheel, and you will undermine your analysis (or at least leave it incomplete) by not considering information or acknowledging positions that are commonly discussed in the field.

By remaining unaware of existing thinking, you choose, in effect, to stand outside of the conversation that others interested in the subject are having. Standing in this sort of intellectual vacuum sometimes appeals to writers who fear that consulting sources will leave them with nothing to say. But it is possible, as this chapter shows, to find a *middle ground* between developing an idea that is entirely independent of what experts have written on a subject and producing a paper that does nothing but repeat other people's ideas. A little research—even if it's only an hour's browse in the reference collection of the library—will virtually always raise the level of what you have to say above what it would have been if you had consulted only the information and opinions that you carry around in your head.

A good rule of thumb for coping with "source anxiety" is to formulate a tentative position on your topic before you consult secondary sources. In other words, give yourself time to do some preliminary thinking. Try writing informally about your topic, analyzing some piece of pertinent information already at your disposal. That way you will have your initial responses written down to weigh in relation to what others have said. Writing of this sort can also help you to select what to look at in the sources you eventually consult.

The Conversation Analogy

Now, let's turn to *the major problem in using sources—a writer leaving the experts he or she cites to speak for themselves*. In this situation, the writer characteristically makes a generalization in his or her own words, juxtaposes it to a quotation or other reference from a secondary source, and assumes that the meaning of the reference will be self-evident. This practice not only leaves the connection between the writer's thinking and his or her source material unstated but also substitutes mere repetition of someone else's viewpoint for a more active interpretation. The source has been allowed to have the final word, with the effect that it stops the discussion and the writer's thinking.

First and foremost, then, you need to do something with the reading. Clarify the meaning of the material you have quoted, paraphrased, or summarized and explain its significance in light of your evolving thesis.

It follows that the first step in using sources effectively is to reject the assumption that sources provide final and complete answers. If they did, there would be no reason for others to continue writing on the subject. As in conversation, we raise ideas for others to respond to. Accepting that no source has the final word does not mean, however, that you should shift from unquestioning approval to the opposite pole and necessarily assume an antagonistic position toward all sources. Indeed, a habitually antagonistic response to others' ideas is just as likely to bring your conversation with your sources to a halt as is the habit of always assuming that the source must have the final word.

Most people would probably agree on the attributes of a really good conversation. There is room for agreement and disagreement, for give and take, among a variety of viewpoints. Generally, people don't deliberately misunderstand each other, but a significant amount of the discussion may go into clarifying one's own as well as others' positions. Such conversations construct a genuinely collaborative *chain* of thinking: Karl builds on what David has said, which induces Jill to respond to Karl's comment, and so forth.

There are, of course, obvious differences between conversing aloud with friends and conversing on paper with sources. As a writer, you need to construct the chain of thinking, orchestrate the exchange of views with and among your sources, and give the conversation direction. A good place to begin in using sources is to recognize that you need not respond to everything another writer says, nor do you need to come up with an entirely original point of view—one that completely revises or refutes the source. You are using sources analytically, for example, when you note that two experiments (or historical accounts, or whatever) are similar but have different priorities or that they ask similar questions in different ways. Building from this kind of observation, you can then analyze what these differences imply.

Ways to Use a Source As a Point of Departure

There are, in any case, many ways of approaching secondary sources, but these ways generally share a common goal: to use the source as a point of departure. Here is a partial list of ways to do that.

- Make as many points as you can about a single representative passage from your source, and then branch out from this center to analyze other passages that "speak" to it in some way. (See "Building a Paper by Analyzing Evidence in Depth: '10 on 1'" in Chapter 5.)

- Use Notice and focus to identify what you find most strange in the source (see Chapter 1); this will help you cultivate your curiosity about the source and find the critical distance necessary to thinking about it.
- Use Looking for Patterns of Repetition and Contrast to identify the most significant organizing contrast in the source (see Chapter 2); this will help you see what the source itself is wrestling with, what is at stake in it.
- Apply an idea in the source to another subject. (See "Applying a Reading as a Lens" in Chapter 4.)
- Uncover the assumptions in the source, and then build upon the source's point of view, extending its implications. (See "Uncovering the Assumptions in a Reading" in Chapter 4.)
- Agree with most of what the source says, but take issue with one small part that you want to modify.
- Identify a contradiction in the source, and explore its implications, without necessarily arriving at a solution.

In using a source as a point of departure you are in effect using it as a stimulus to have an idea. As you may recall from the discussion of what it means to have an idea in Chapter 1, most strong analytical ideas launch you into a process of resolving problems and bringing competing positions into some kind of alignment. They locate you where there is something to negotiate, where you are required not just to list answers but also to ask questions, make choices, and engage in reasoning about the significance of your evidence.

If you quote with the aim of conversing with your sources rather than allowing them to do your thinking for you, you will discover that sources can promote rather than stifle your ability to have ideas. So try to think of sources not as answers but as voices inviting you into a community of interpretation, discussion, and debate. As the discussion of reporting versus analyzing in the "Voices from Across the Curriculum" box demonstrates, this practice is common to different academic disciplines.

VOICES FROM ACROSS THE CURRICULUM

Reporting Versus Analyzing in Scientific Experiments

There is a big difference between simply reporting on what has been done in a scientific venture and analyzing and evaluating the venture. One of the problems with trying to *read* critical analyses of scientific work is that few scientists want to be in print criticizing their colleagues. That is, for political reasons scientists who write reviews are likely to soften their criticism or even avoid it entirely by reporting the findings of others simply and directly. However, by definition such a review is not critical. That author stakes out no particular point of view and thus does not have to defend anything.

What I want from students in molecular biology is a critical analysis of the work they have researched. This can take several forms.

First, *analyze* what was done. What were the assumptions (hypotheses) going into the experiment? What was the logic of the experimental design? What were the results?

Second, *evaluate* the results and conclusions. Here, it's even appropriate to use the first person. *You* are commenting on the field. Foremost, how well do the results support the conclusions? What alternative interpretations are there? What additional experiments could be done to strengthen or refute the argument? This is hard, no doubt, but it is what you should be doing every time you read anything in science or otherwise.

Third, *synthesize* the results and interpretations of a given experiment in the context of the field. How does this study inform other studies? Even though practicing scientists are hesitant to do this in print, everyone does it informally in journal clubs held usually on a weekly basis in every lab all over the world.

—Bruce Wightman, Professor of Biology

Plagiarism and the Logic of Citation

It is impossible to discuss the rationale for citing sources without reference to plagiarism, even though the primary reason for including citations is not to prove that you haven't cheated. It's essential that you give credit where it's due as a courtesy to your readers. Along with educating readers about who has said what, citations enable them to find out more about a given position and to pursue other discussions on the subject. Nonetheless, plagiarism is an important issue: academic integrity matters. And because the stakes are very high if you are caught plagiarizing, we think it necessary to pause in order to discuss how to avoid it.

In recent years there has been a significant rise in the number of plagiarism cases nationally. Many commentators blame the Internet, with its easily accessible, easy to cut-and-paste information, for increasing the likelihood of plagiarism. Others cite a lack of clarity about what plagiarism is and why it is a serious problem. So, let's start by clarifying.

Most people have some idea of what plagiarism is. You already know that it's against the rules to buy a paper from an Internet "paper mill" or to download others' words verbatim and hand them in as your own thinking. And you probably know that even if you change a few words and rearrange the sentence structure, you still need to acknowledge the source. By way of formal definition, plagiarism (as one handbook puts it) gives "the impression that you have written or thought something that you have in fact borrowed from someone else" (Joseph Gibaldi, *MLA Handbook for Writers of Research Papers*, Fifth edition. New York: MLA, 1999, p. 30). It is a form of theft and fraud. Borrowing from someone else, by the way, also includes taking and not acknowledging words and ideas from your friends or your parents. Put another way, any assignment with your name on it signifies that you are the author—that the words and ideas are yours—with any exceptions indicated by source citations and, if you're quoting, by quotation marks.

Knowing what plagiarism is, however, doesn't guarantee that you'll know how to avoid it. Is it okay, for example, to cobble together a series of summaries and paraphrases in a paragraph, provided you include the authors in a bibliography at the end of the paper? Or how about if you insert a single footnote at the end of the paragraph? The answer is that both are still plagiarism, because your reader can't tell where your thinking starts and others' thinking stops. As a basic rule of thumb, *"Readers must be able to tell as they are reading your paper exactly what information came from which source and what information is your contribution to the paper"* (Christine A. Hult, *Researching and Writing Across the Curriculum*. Boston: Allyn and Bacon, 1996, p. 203). More on this later.

Why Does Plagiarism Matter?

A recent survey indicated that 53 percent of Who's Who High Schoolers thought that plagiarism was no big deal (Sally Cole and Elizabeth Kiss, "What Can We Do About Student Cheating?" *About Campus*, May–June 2000, p. 6). So why should institutions of higher learning care about it? Here are two great reasons:

- Plagiarism poisons the environment. Students who don't cheat get alienated by students who do and get away with it, and faculty can become distrustful of students and even disillusioned about teaching when constantly driven to track down students' sources. It's a lot easier, by the way, than most students think for faculty to recognize language and ideas that are not the student's own. And now there are all those search engines provided by firms like Turnitin.com that have been generated in response to the Internet paper-mill boom. Who wants another cold war?
- Plagiarism defeats the purpose of going to college, which is learning how to think. You can't learn to think by just copying others' ideas; you need to learn to trust your own intelligence. Students' panic about deadlines and their misunderstandings about assignments sometimes spur plagiarism. It's a good bet that your professors would much rather take requests for help and give extra time on assignments than have to go through the anguish of confronting students about plagiarized work.

So, plagiarism gets in the way of trust, fairness, intellectual development, and, ultimately, the attitude toward learning that sets the tone for a college or university community.

Frequently Asked Questions (FAQs) about Plagiarism

Is it still plagiarism if I didn't intentionally copy someone else's work and present it as my own; that is, if I plagiarized it by accident?

Yes, it is still plagiarism. Colleges and universities put the burden of responsibility on students for knowing what plagiarism is and then making the effort necessary to avoid it. Leaving out the quotation marks around someone else's words or omitting the attribution after a summary of someone else's theory may be just a mistake—a matter of inadequate documentation—but faculty can only judge what you turn in to them, not what you intended.

If I include a list of works consulted at the end of my paper, doesn't that cover it?

No. A works-cited list (bibliography) tells your readers what you read but leaves them in the dark about how and where this material has been used in your paper. Putting one or more references at the end of a paragraph containing source material is a version of the same problem. The solution is to cite the source at the point that you quote or paraphrase or summarize it. To be even clearer about what comes from where, also use what are called in-text attributions. See the next FAQ on these.

What is the best way to help my readers distinguish between what my sources are saying and what I'm saying?

Be overt. Tell your readers in the text of your paper, not just in citations, when you are drawing on someone else's words, ideas, or information. Do this with phrases like "According to X . . ." or as noted in X . . ."—so-called in-text attributions.

Are there some kinds of information that I do not need to document?

Yes. Common knowledge and facts you can find in almost any encyclopedia or basic reference text generally don't need to be documented (that is, John F. Kennedy became president of the United States in 1960). This distinction can get a little tricky because it isn't always obvious what is and is not common knowledge. Often, you need to spend some time in a discipline before you discover what others take to be known to all. When in doubt, cite the source.

If I put the information from my sources into my own words, do I still need to include citations?

Yes. Sorry, but rewording someone else's idea doesn't make it your idea. Paraphrasing is a useful activity because it helps you to better understand what you are reading, but paraphrases and summaries have to be documented and carefully distinguished from ideas and information you are representing as your own.

If I don't actually know anything about the subject, is it okay to hand in a paper that is taken entirely from various sources?

It's okay if (1) you document the borrowings and (2) the assignment called for summary. Properly documented summarizing is better than plagiarizing, but most assignments call for something more. Often comparing and contrasting your sources will begin to give you ideas, so that you can have something to contribute. If you're really stumped, go see the professor.

You will also reduce the risk of plagiarism if you consult sources after—not before—you have done some preliminary thinking on the subject. If you have become somewhat invested in your own thoughts on the matter, you will be able to use the sources in a more active way, in effect, making them part of a dialogue.

Is it plagiarism if I include things in my paper that I thought of with another student or a member of my family?

Most academic behavior codes, under the category called "collusion," allow for students' cooperative efforts only with the explicit consent of the instructor. The same general rule goes for plagiarizing yourself—that is, for submitting the same paper in more than one class. If you have questions about what constitutes collusion in a particular class, be sure to ask your professor.

What about looking at secondary sources when my professor hasn't asked me to? Is this a form of cheating?

It can be a form of cheating if the intent of the assignment was to get you to develop a particular kind of thinking skill. In this case, looking at others' ideas may actually retard your learning process and leave you feeling that you couldn't possibly learn to arrive at ideas on your own.

Professors usually look favorably on students who are willing to take the time to do extra reading on a subject, but it is essential that, even in class discussion, you make it clear that you have consulted outside sources. To conceal that fact is to present others' ideas as your own. Even in class discussion, if you bring up an idea you picked up on the Internet, be sure to say so explicitly.

Call for Papers

Write Now! welcomes submissions for publication in next year's issue. Each year, student essays written for Brandeis University Writing Seminars are published in this volume in recognition of their extraordinary merit. Cash prizes are awarded to the three essays that receive the most votes from our panel of judges.

If you are interested in submitting your essay for consideration, please email your UWS instructor and provide him or her with a digital copy of your essay in .doc, .docx, or .rtf format. You should also include the following information:

- Your name, campus address, and campus phone number
- Your summer address and summer phone number
- An email address that you will be able to check regularly over the summer
- Your UWS instructor's name, and the course and section number of your UWS

Instructors should submit essays to: jaustincypert@gmail.com. If you have any further questions or concerns, please send an email to the current editor of *Write Now!*, Jodie Austin, at this address. Good luck, and remember that your essay might be the one to appear next in this volume.